BY THE SEA

A Nautical Picture Book

Raeka Harding

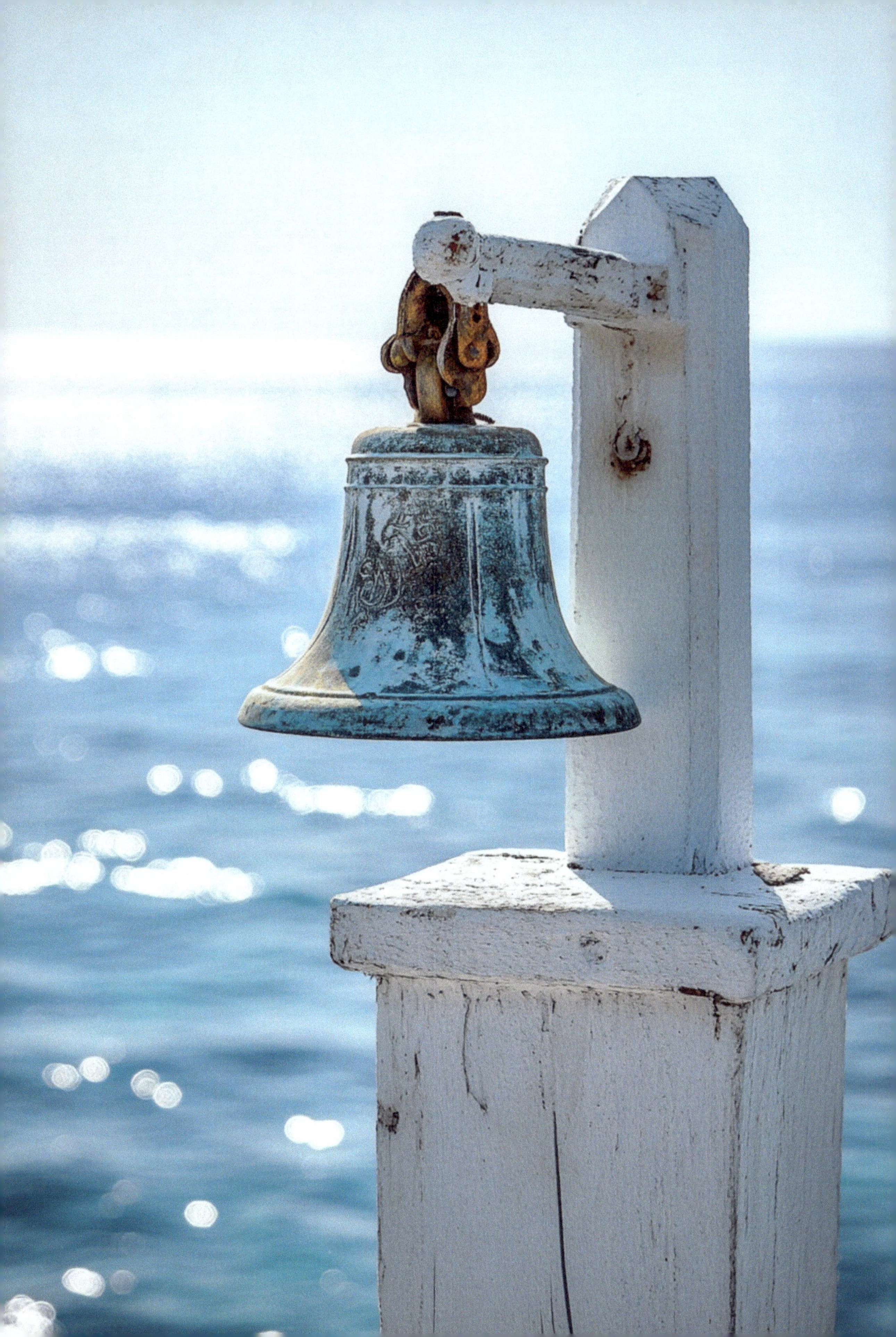

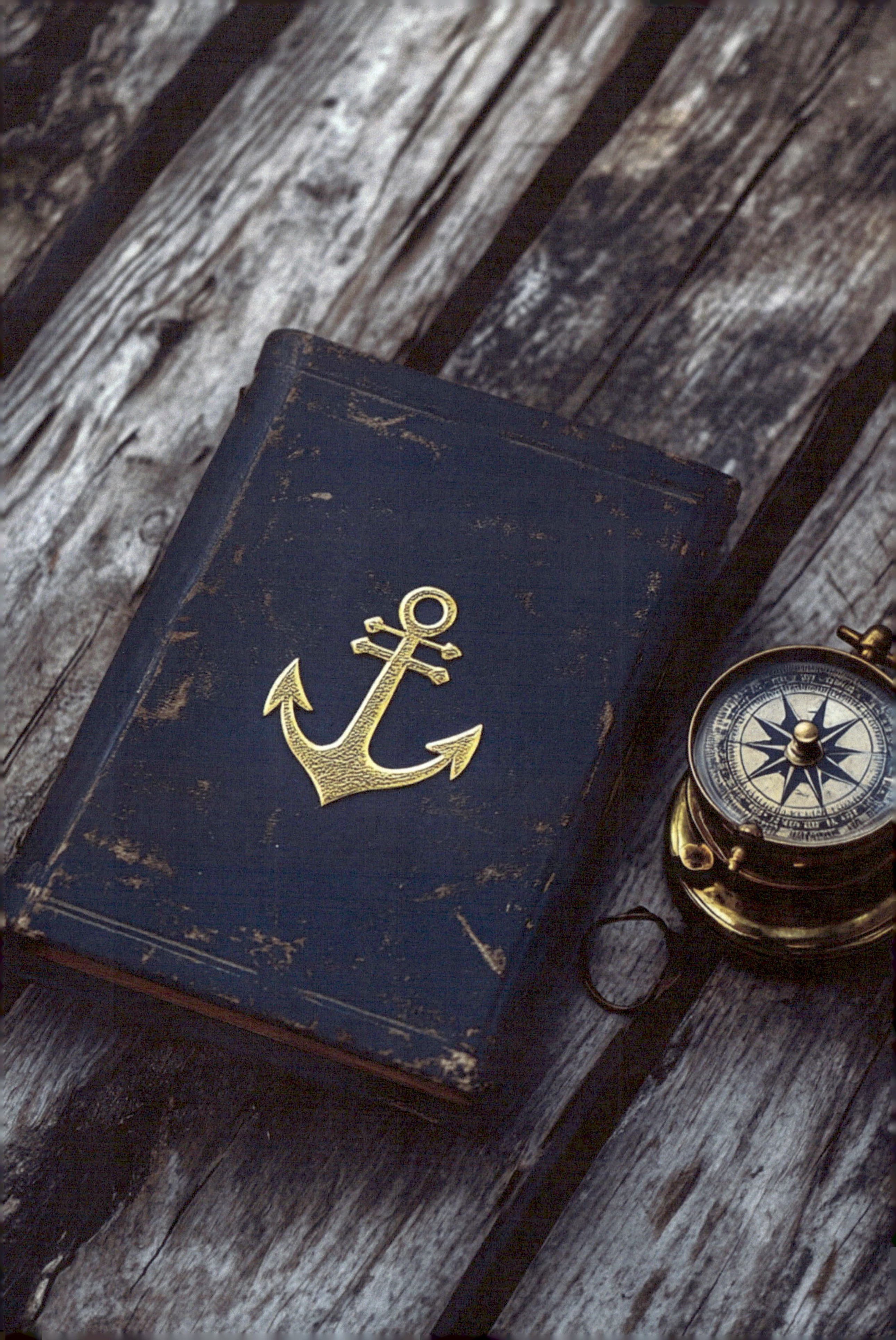

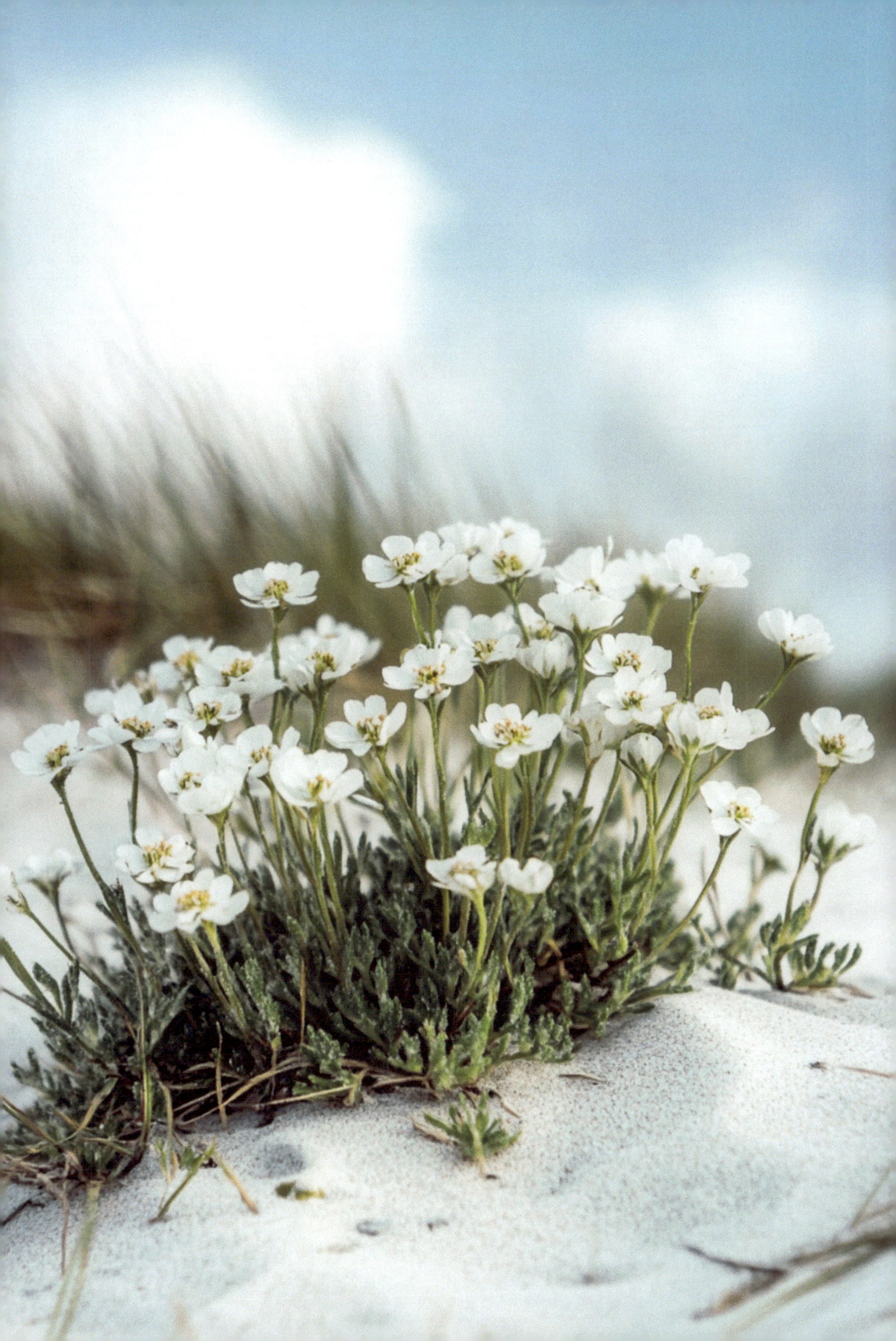

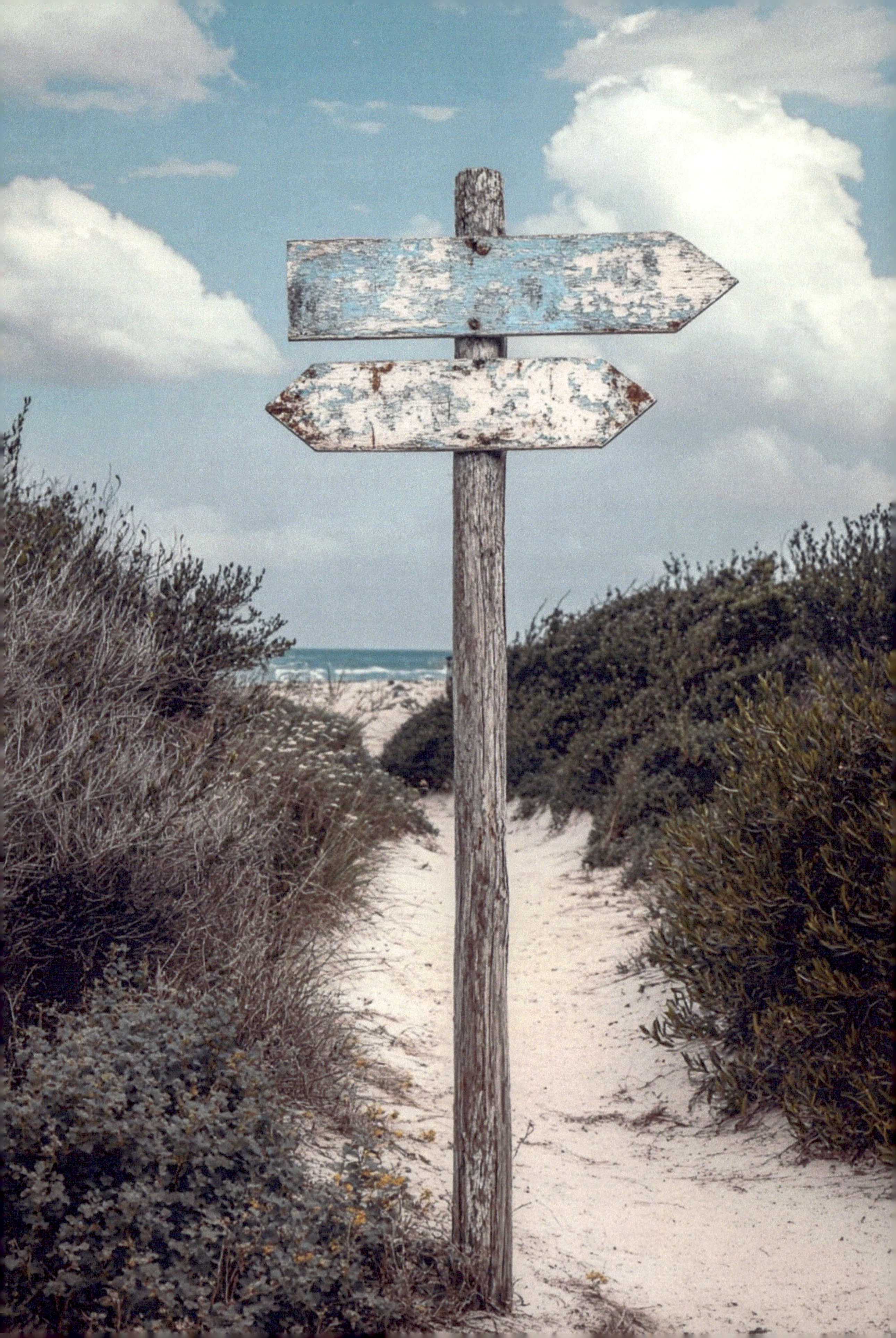

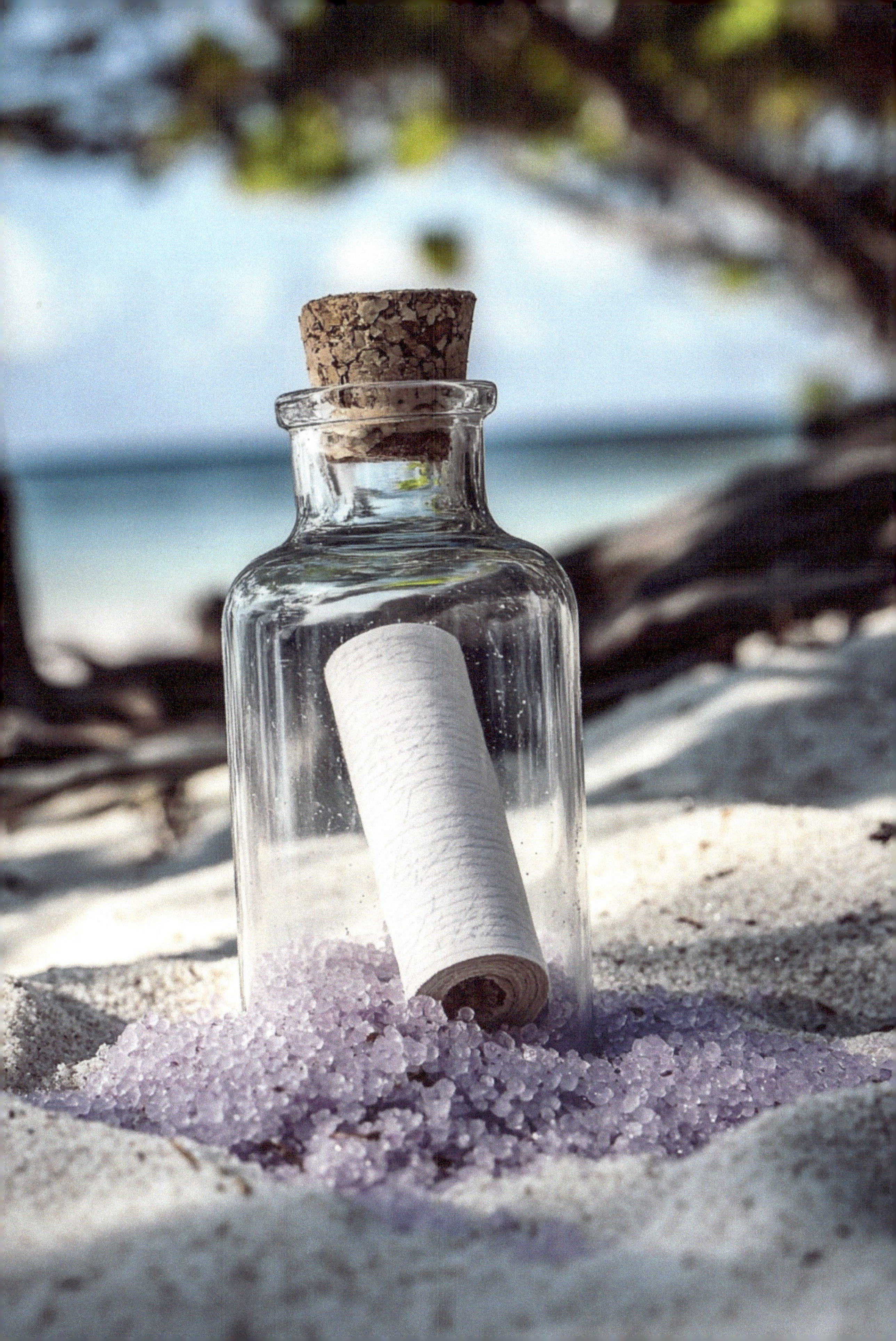

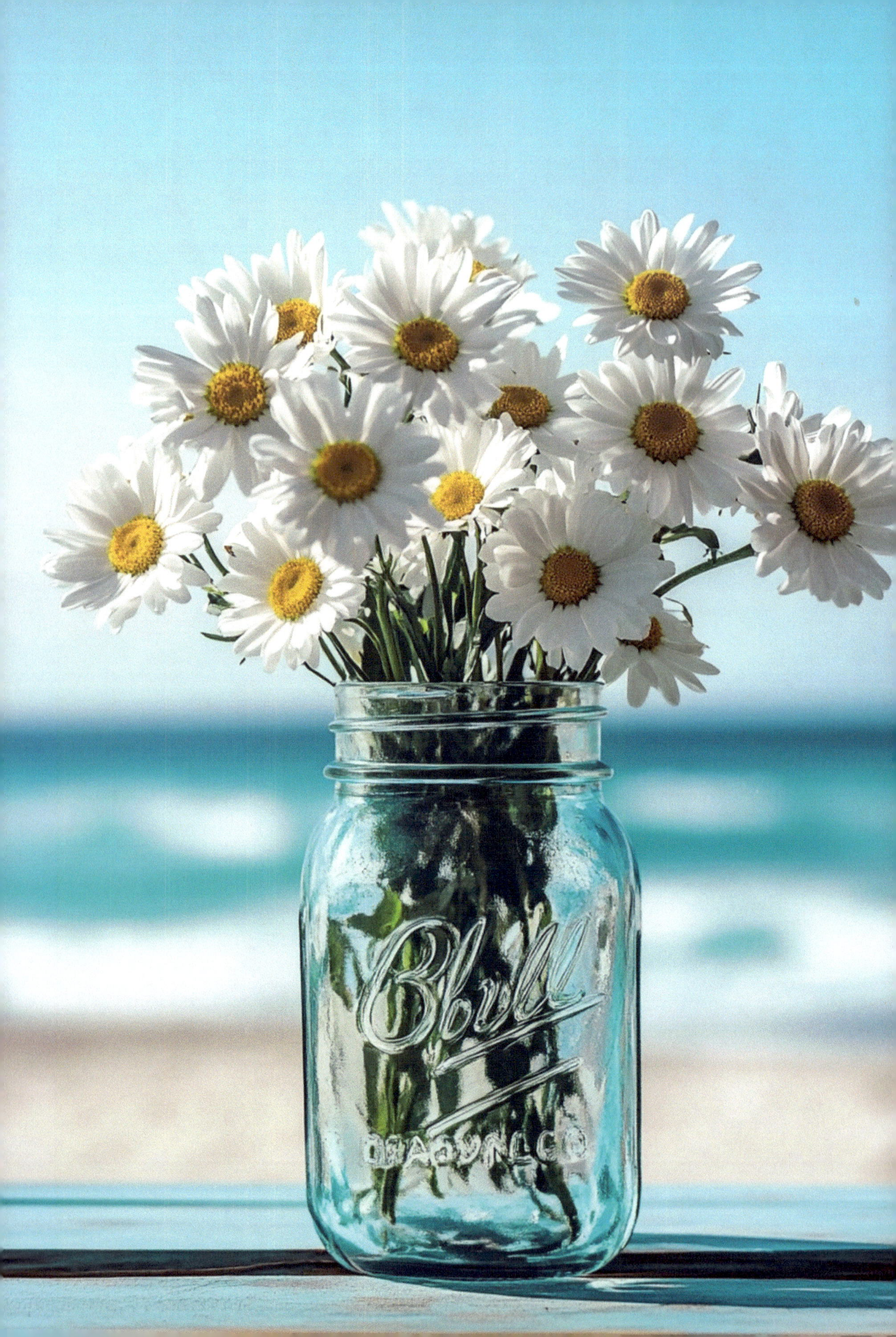

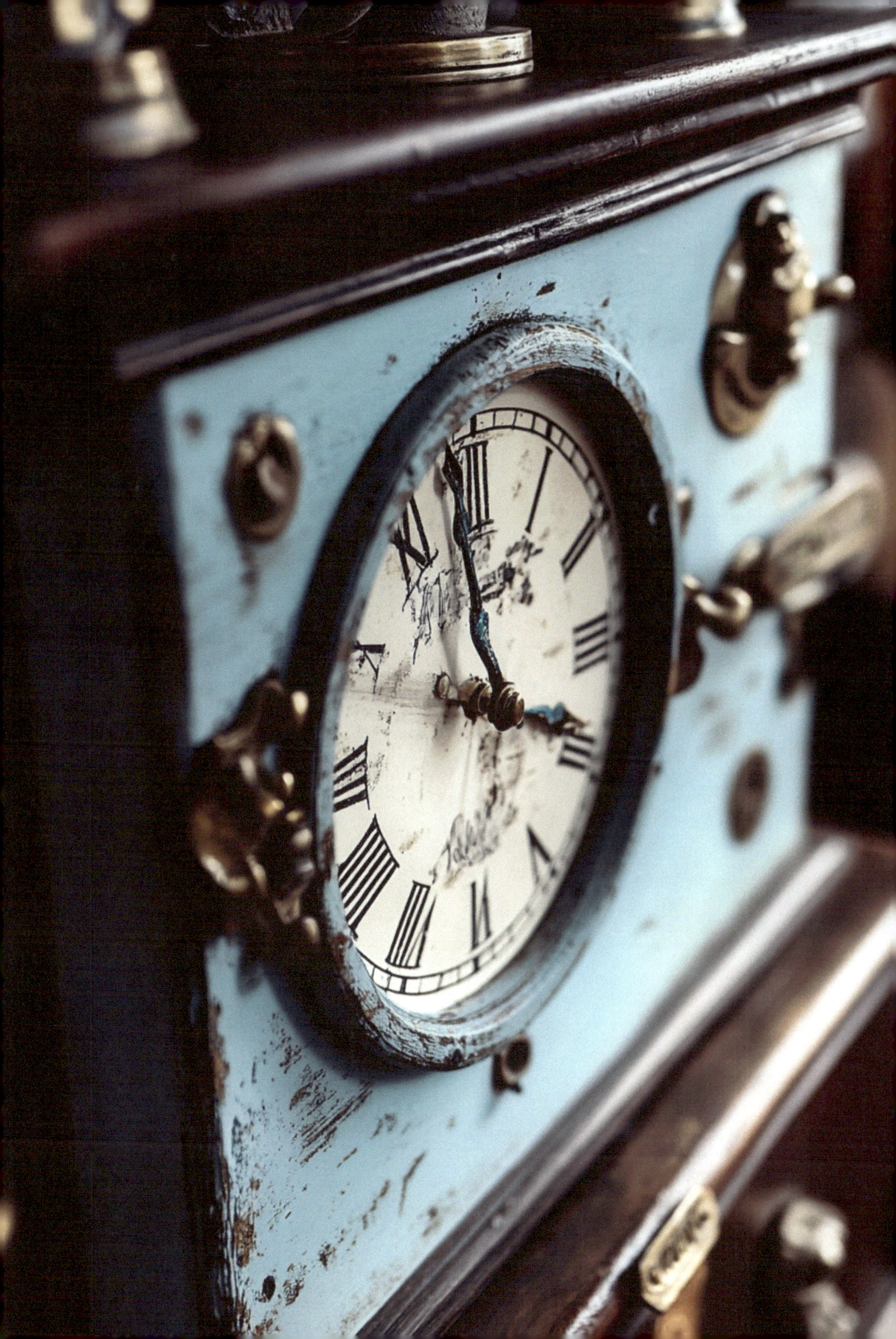

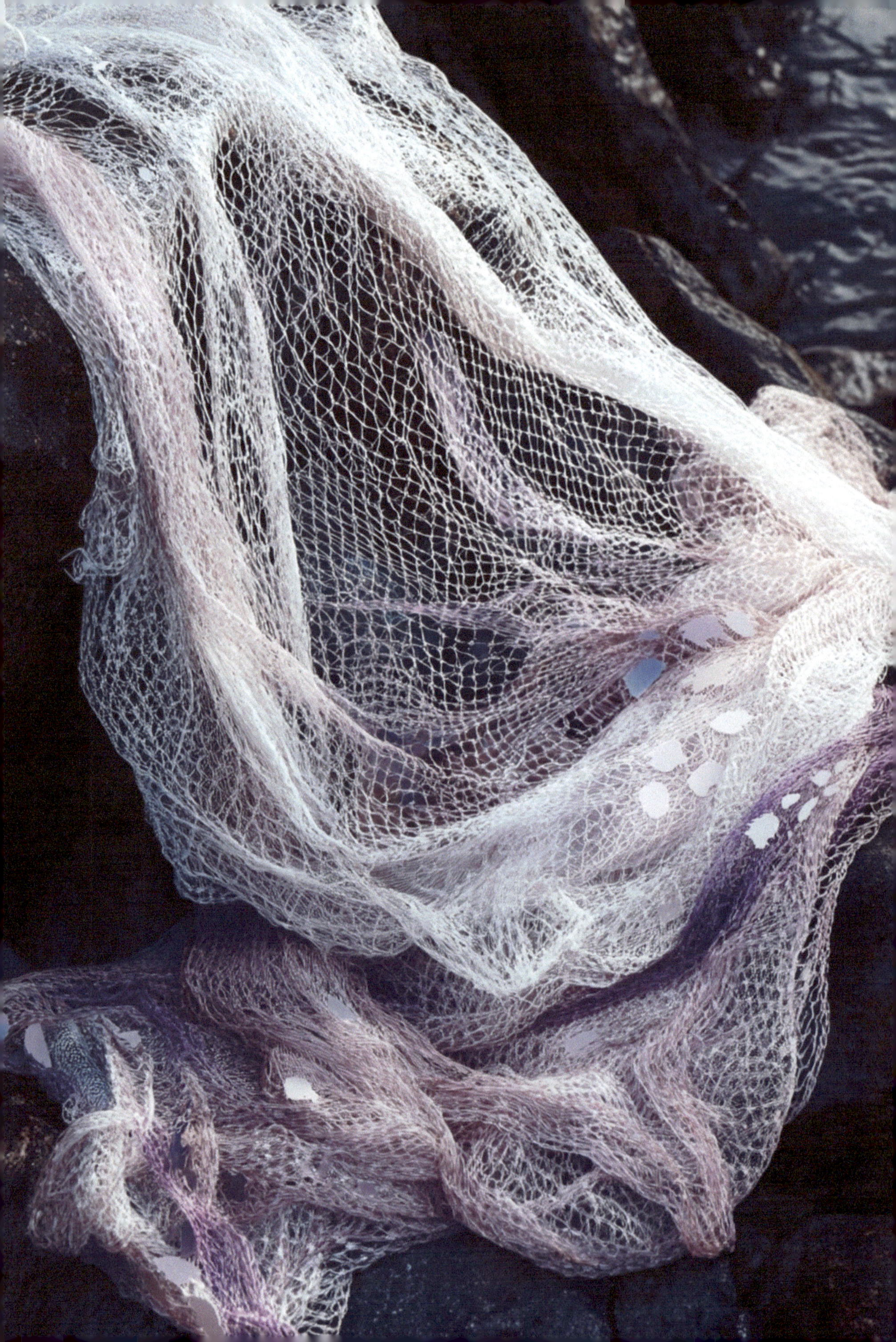

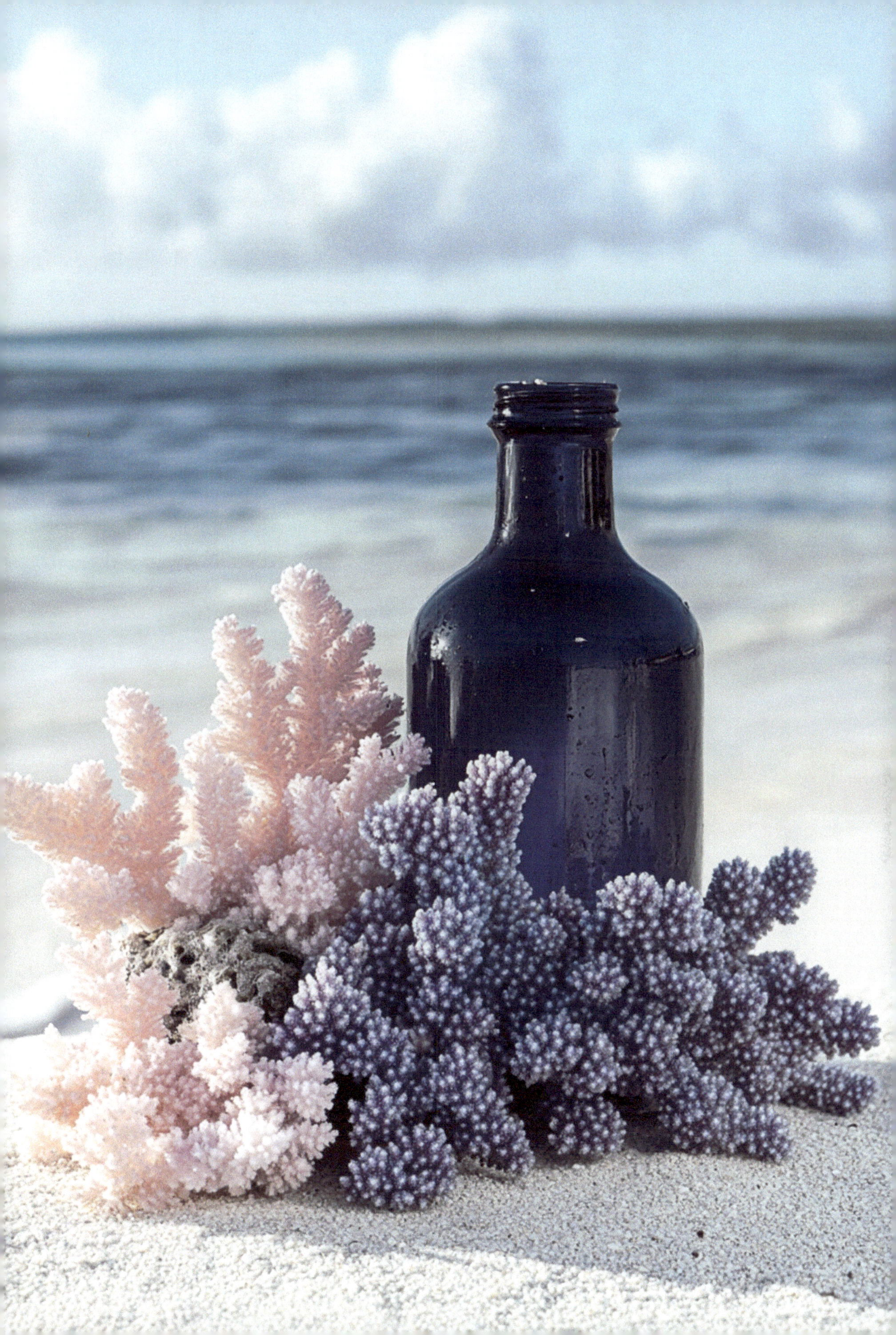

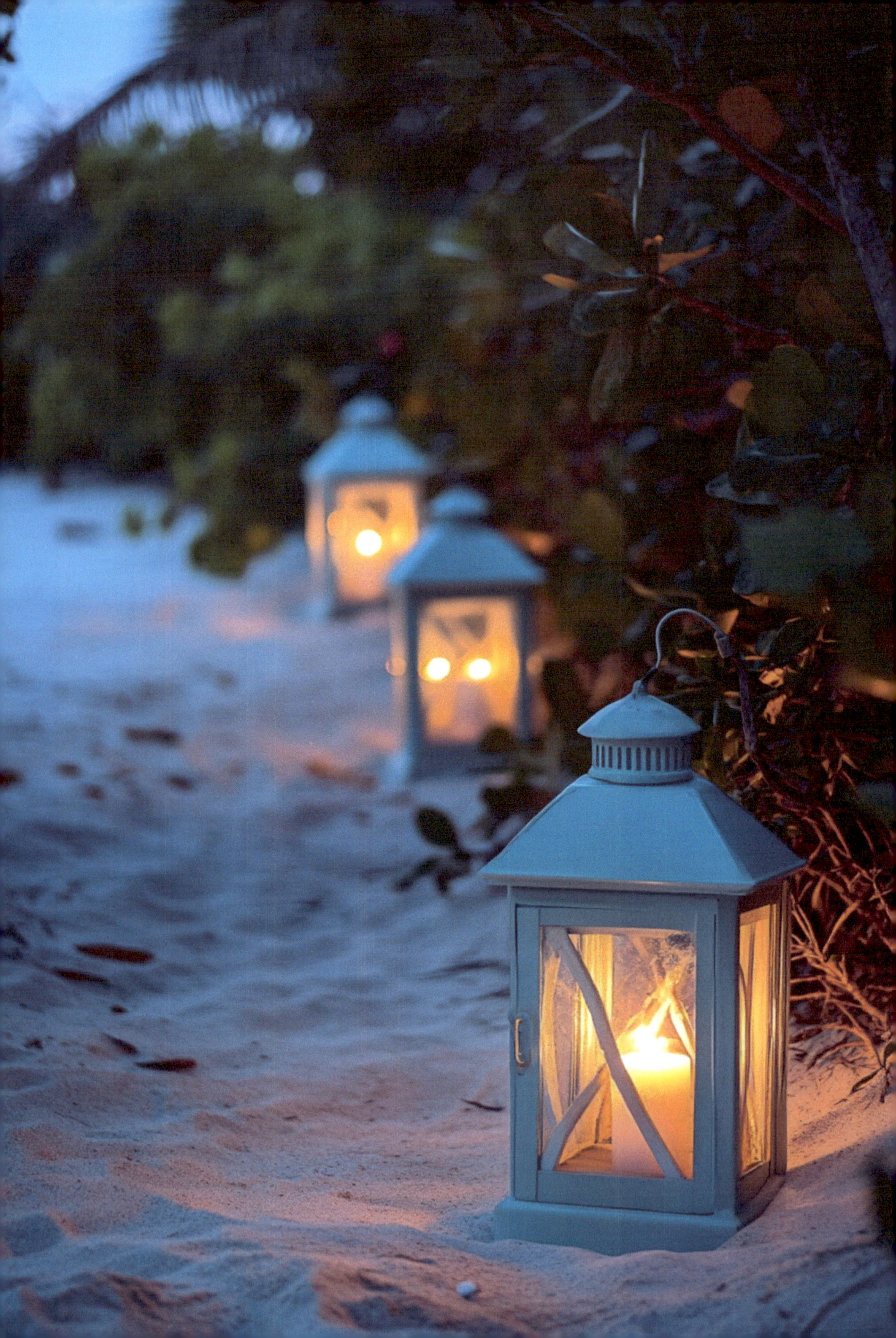

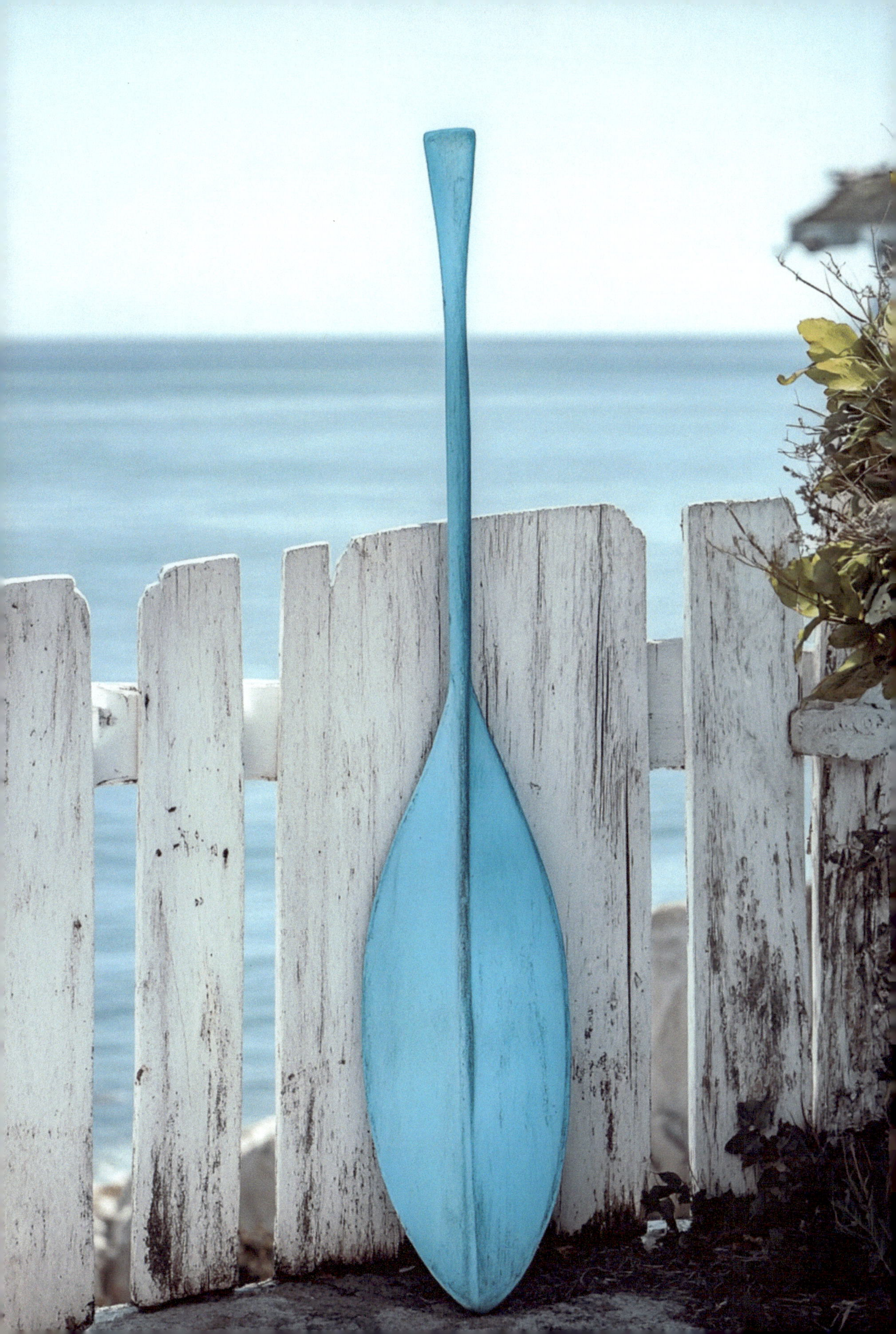

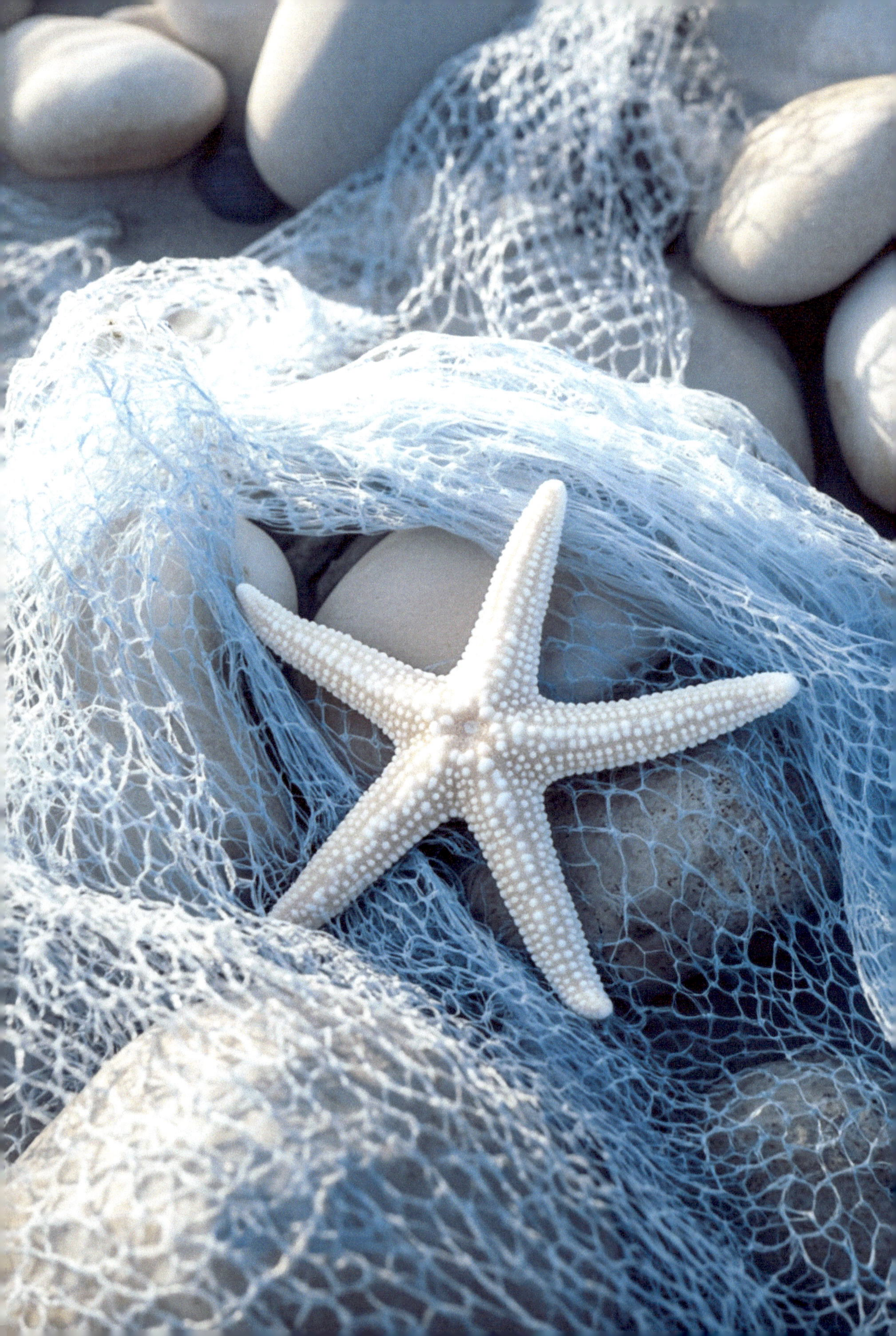

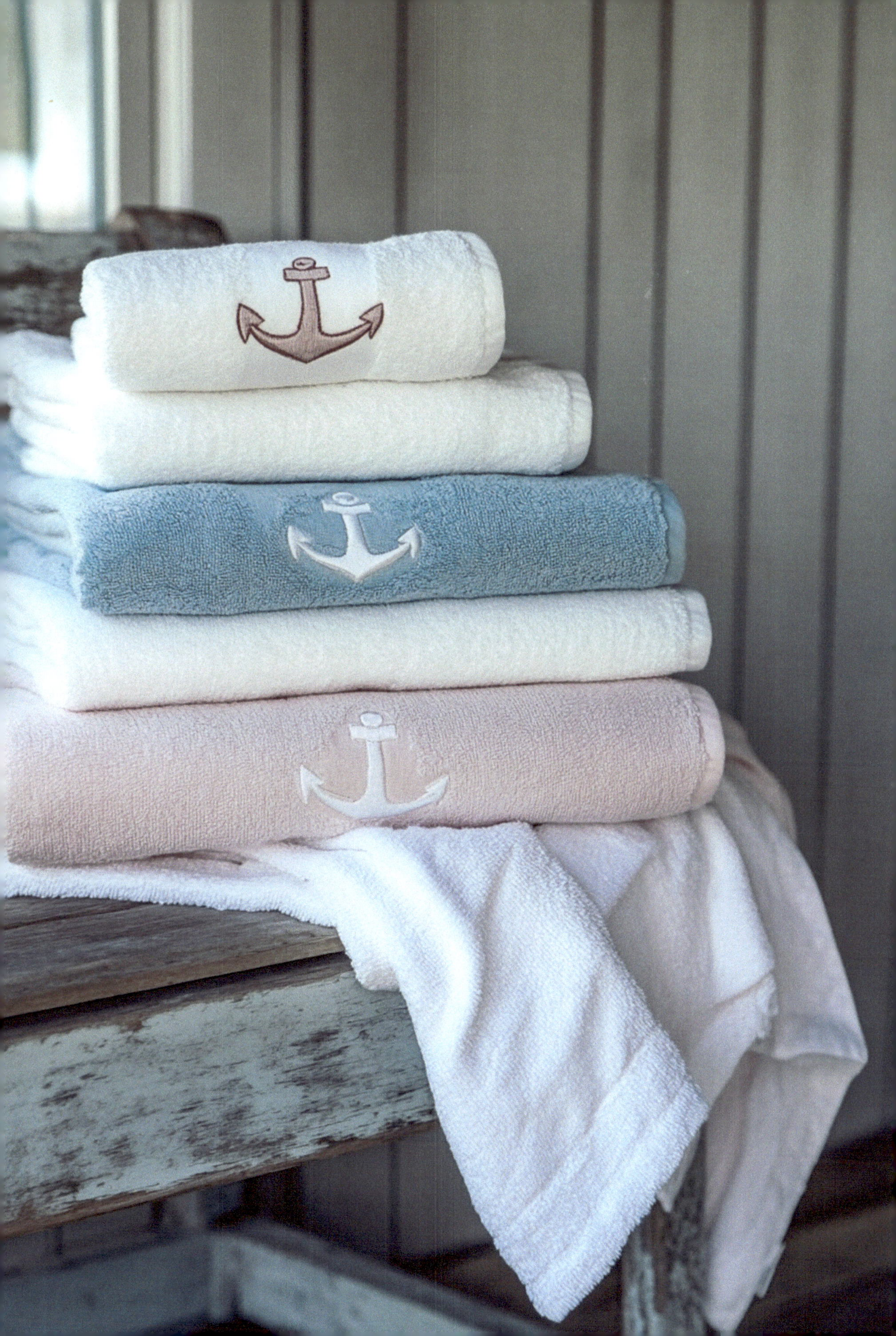

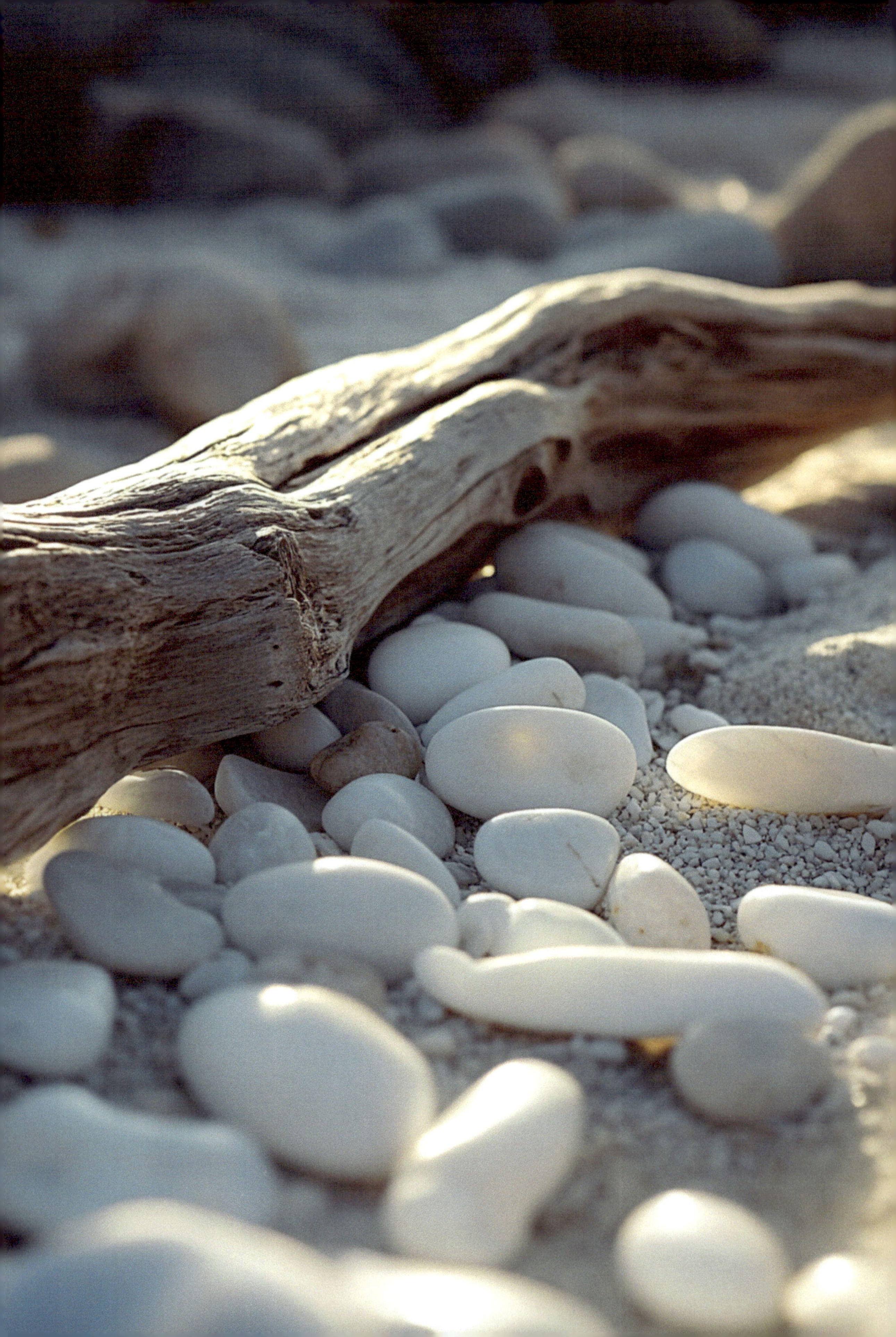

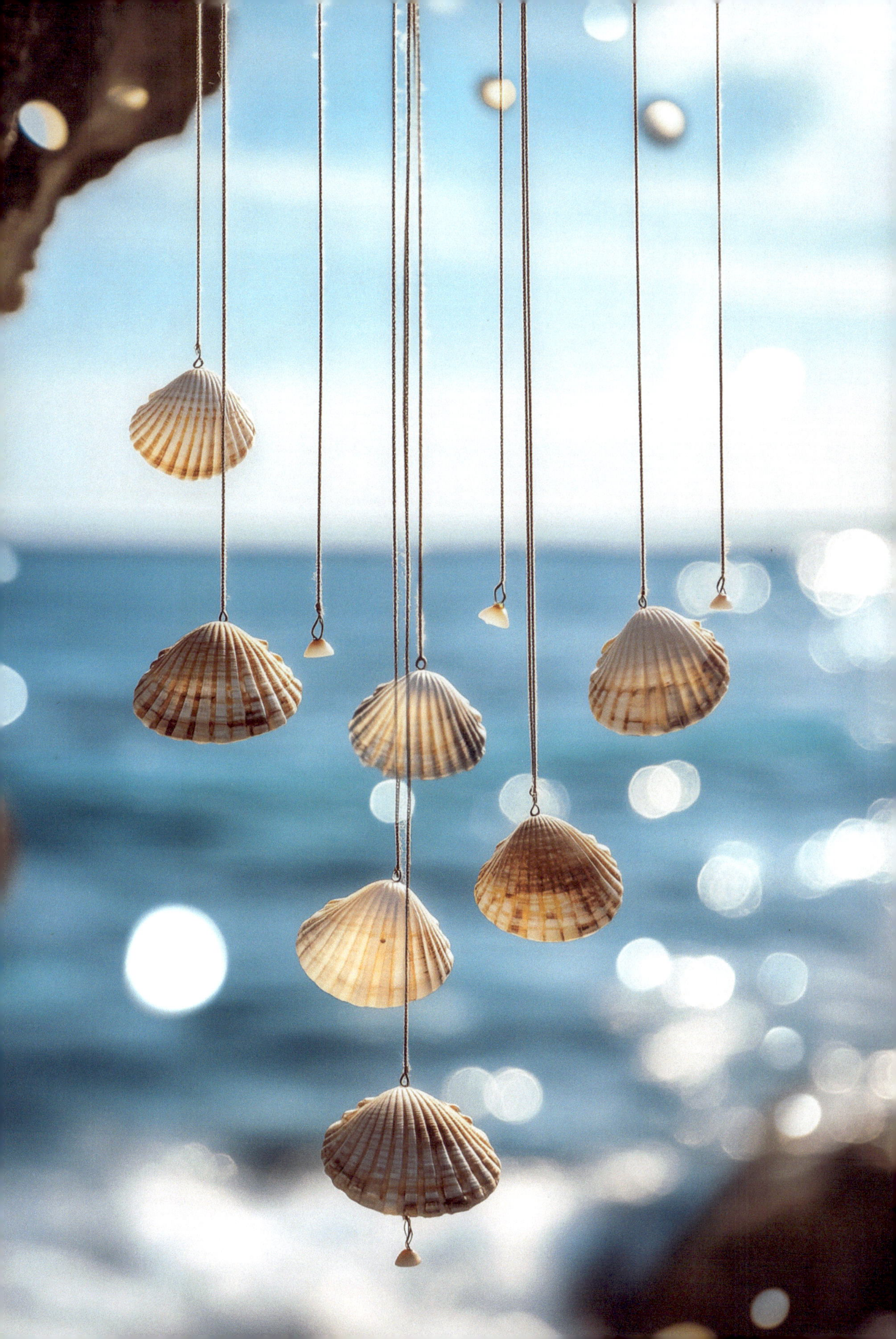

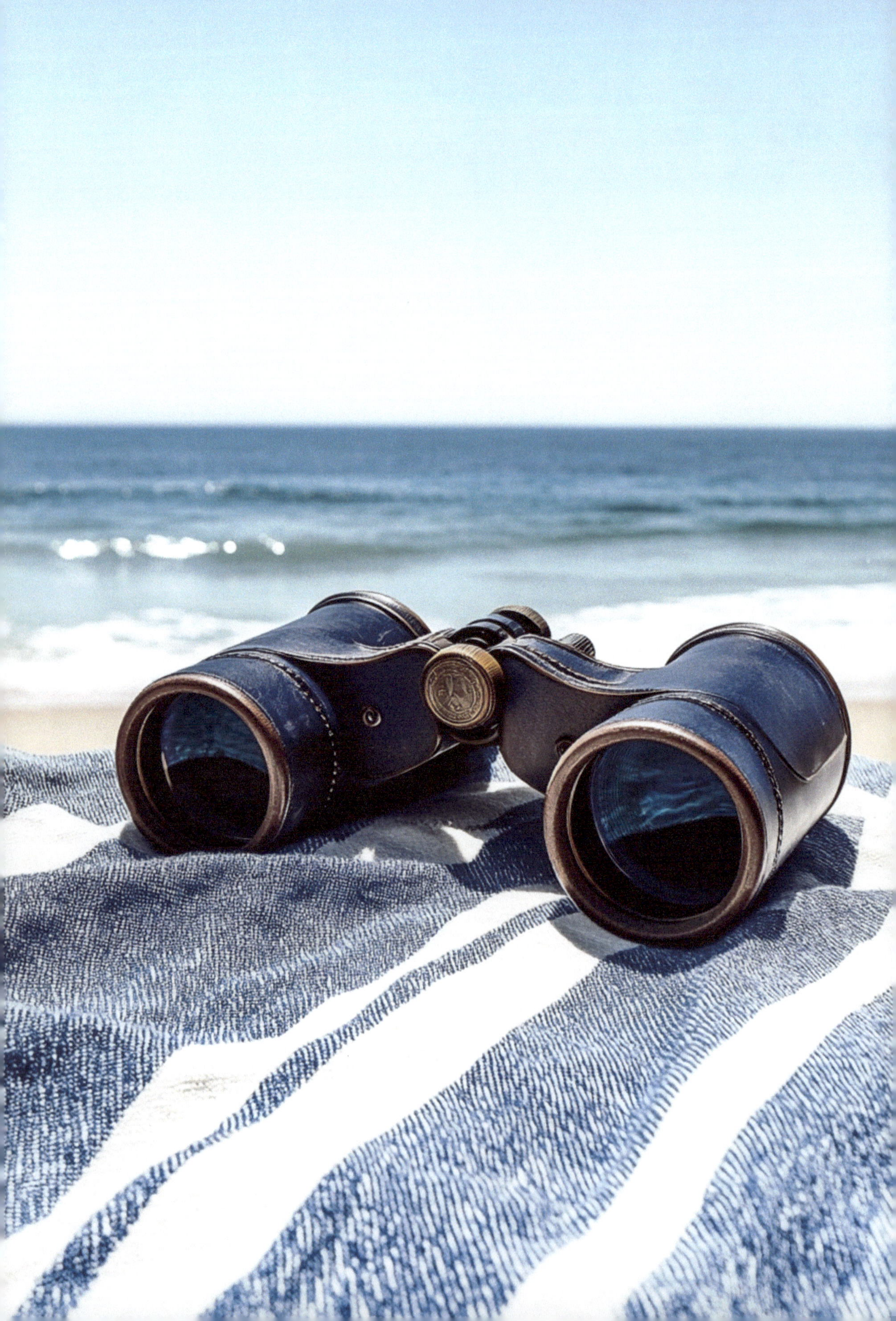

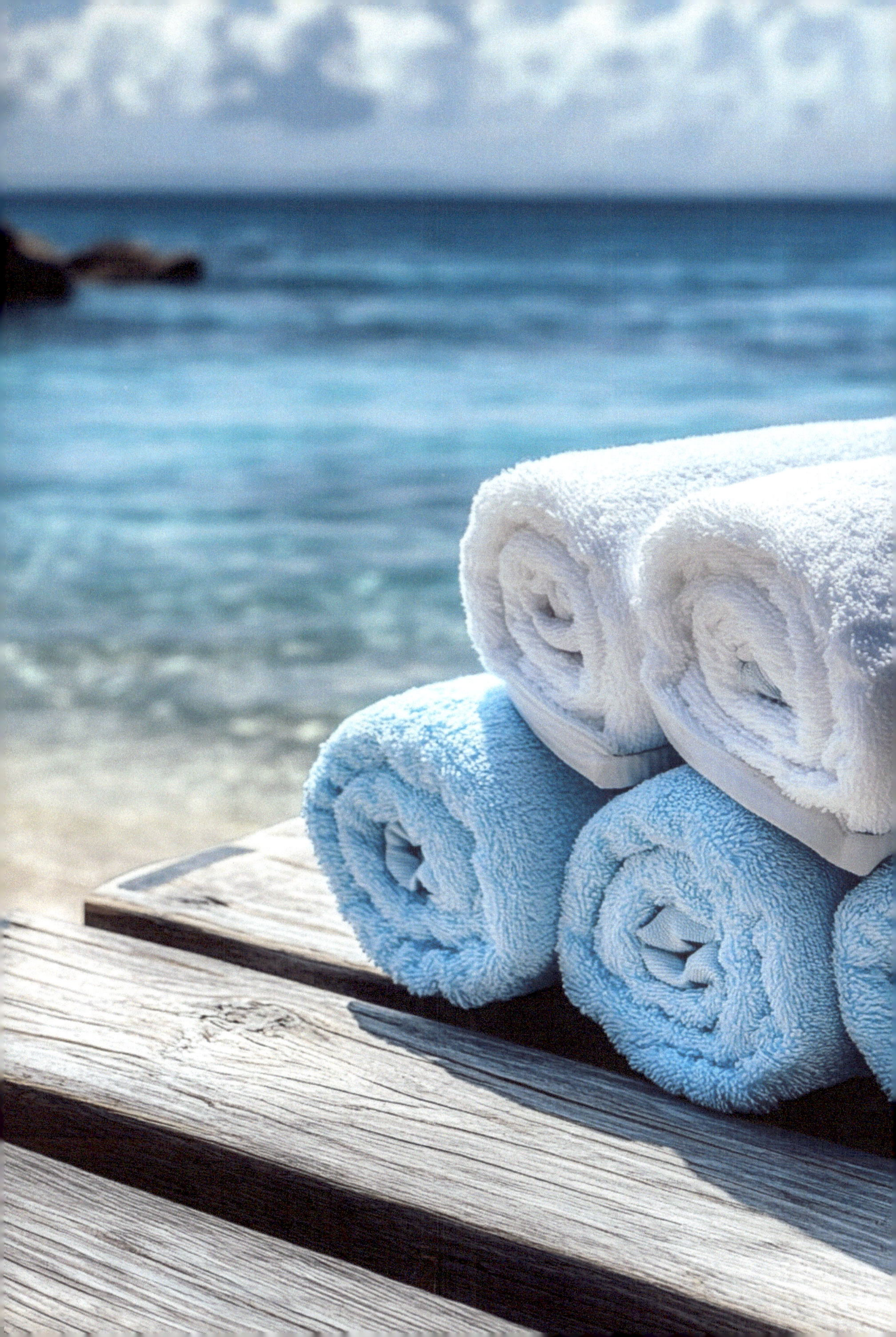

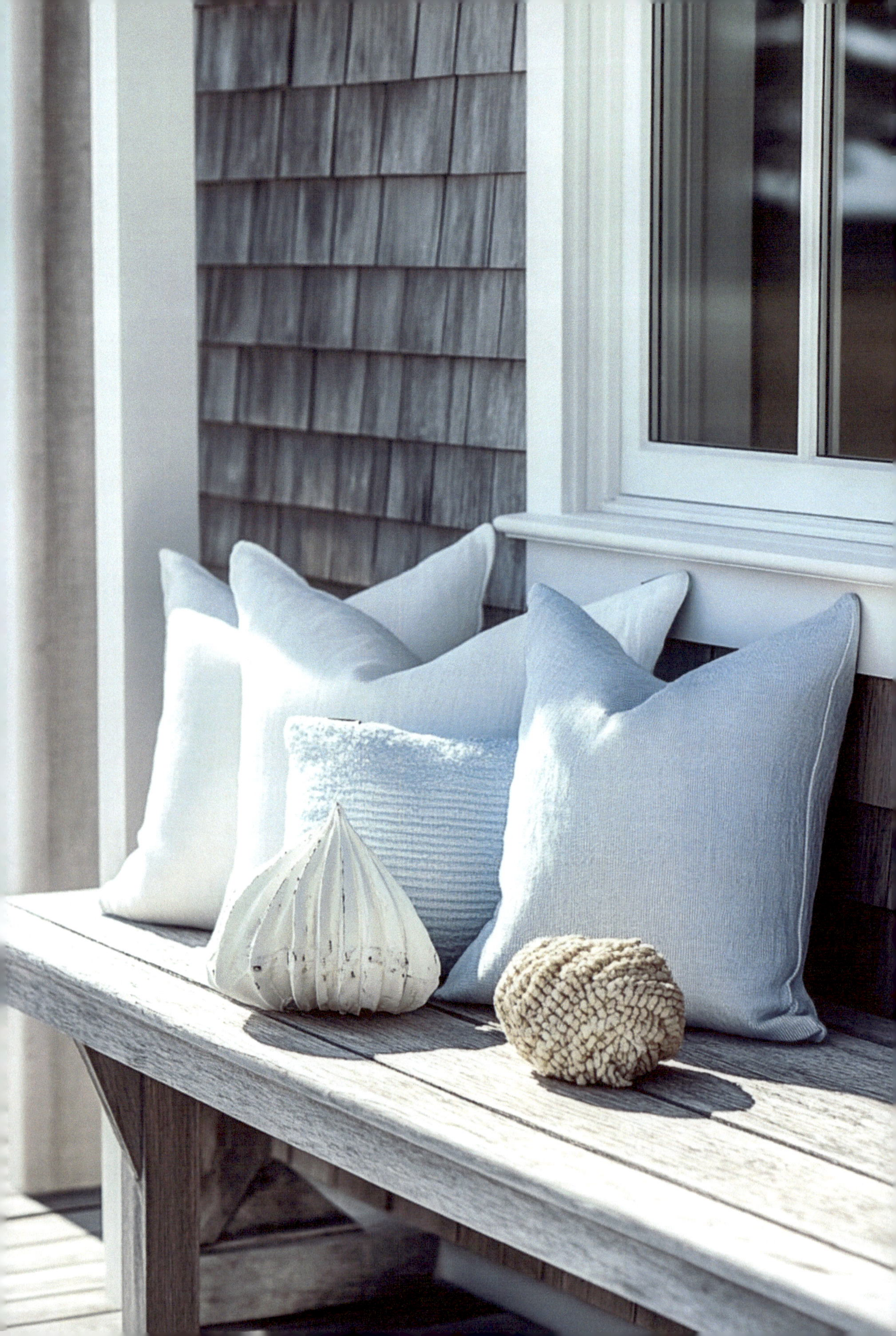

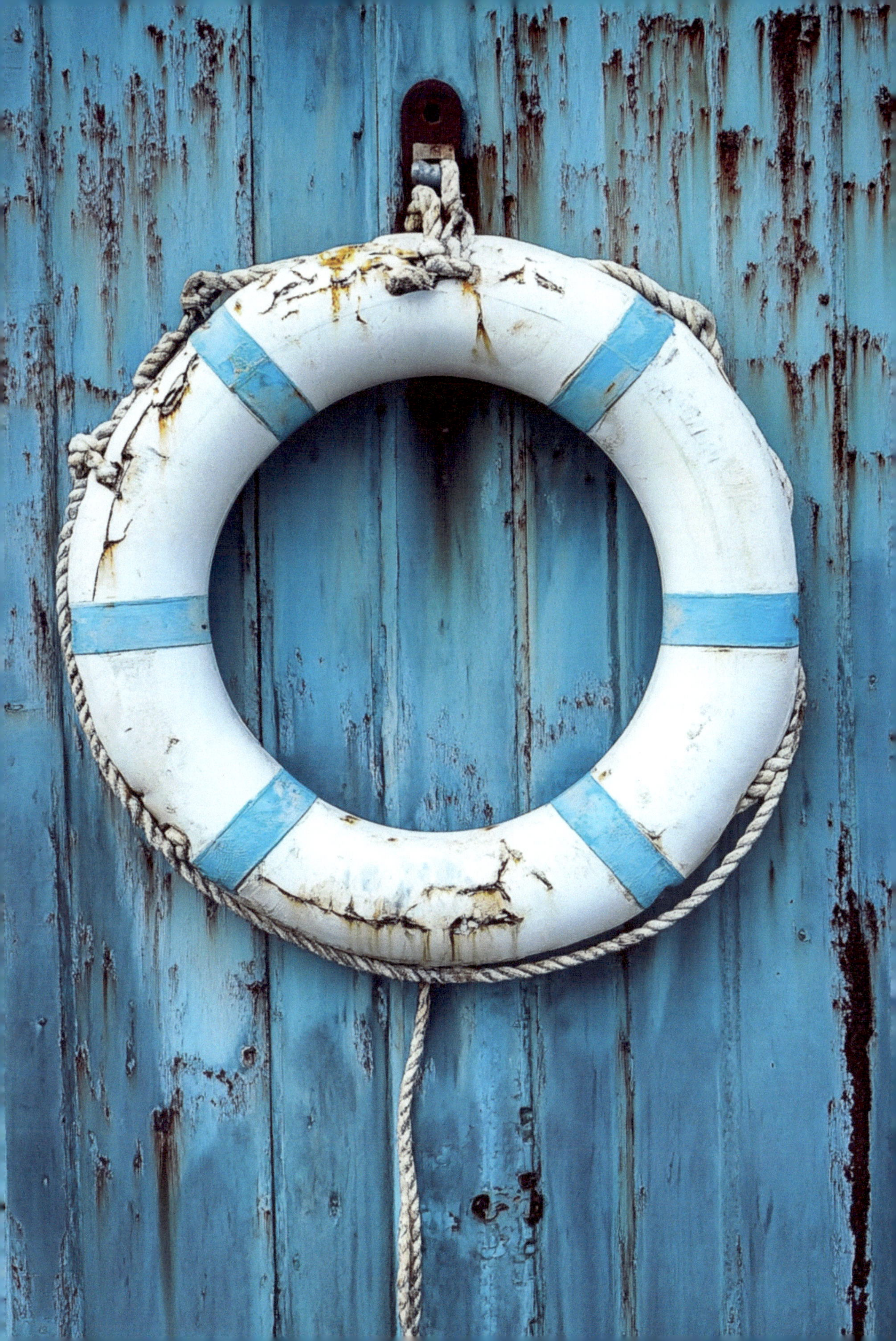

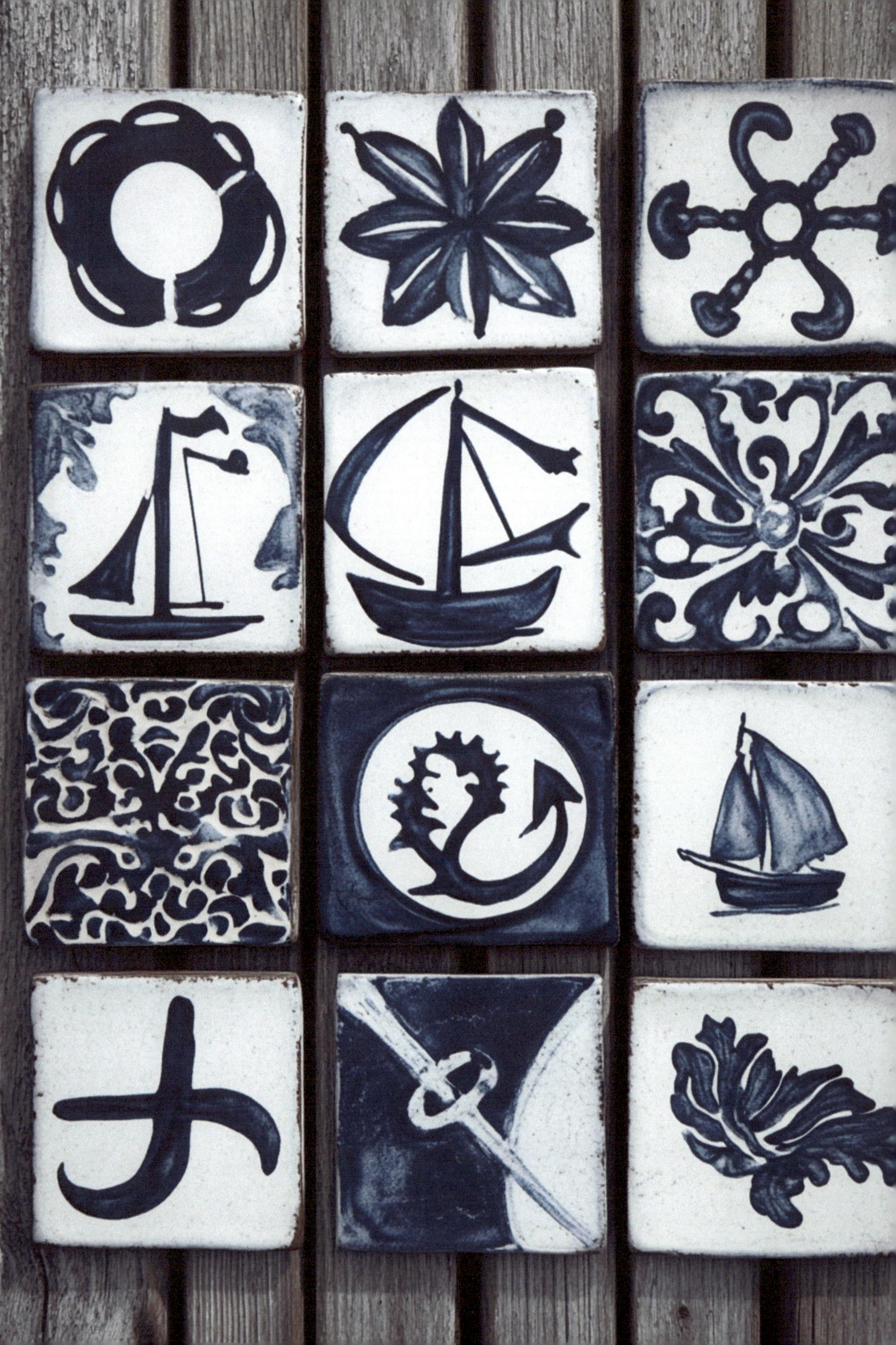

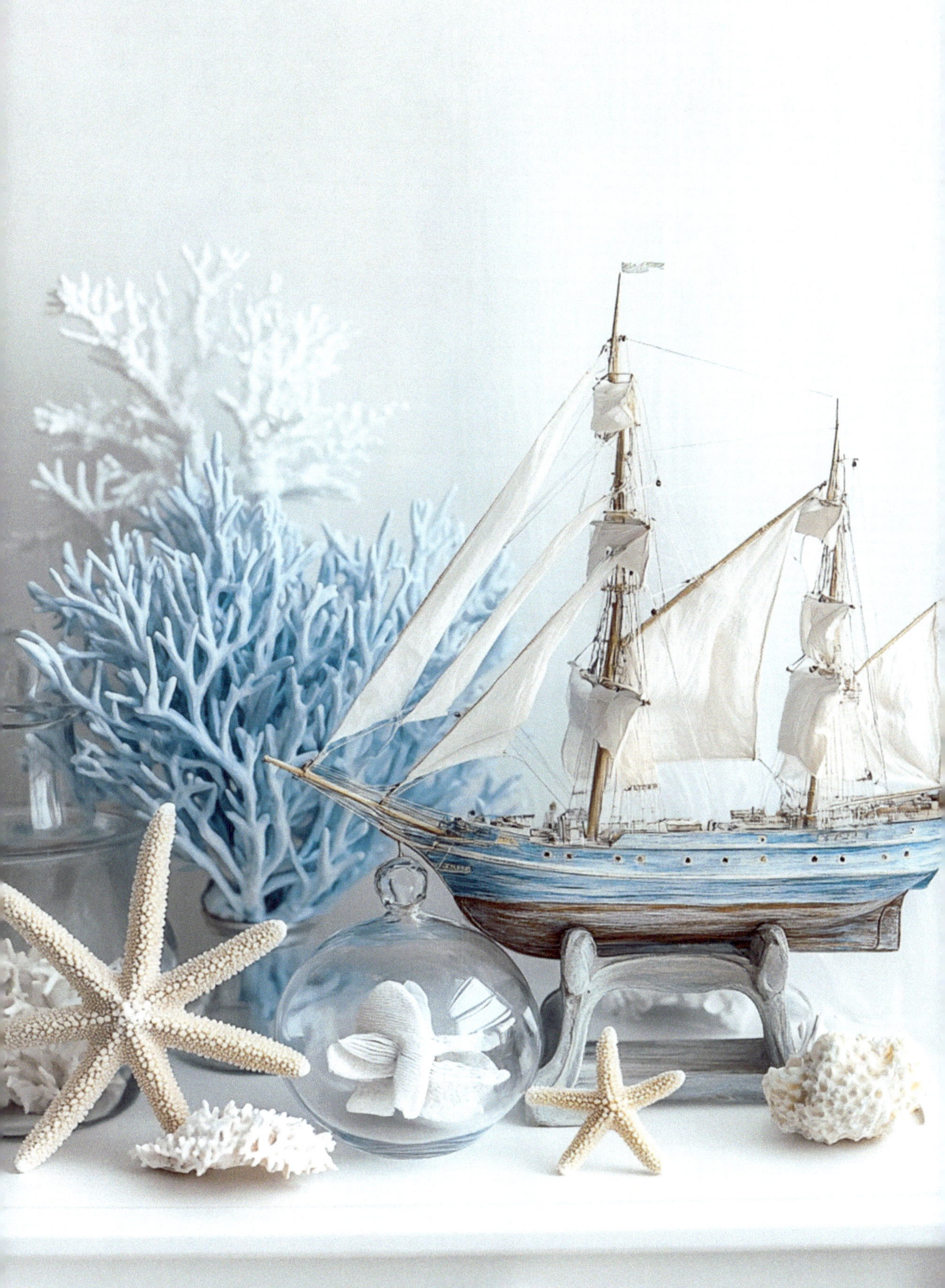

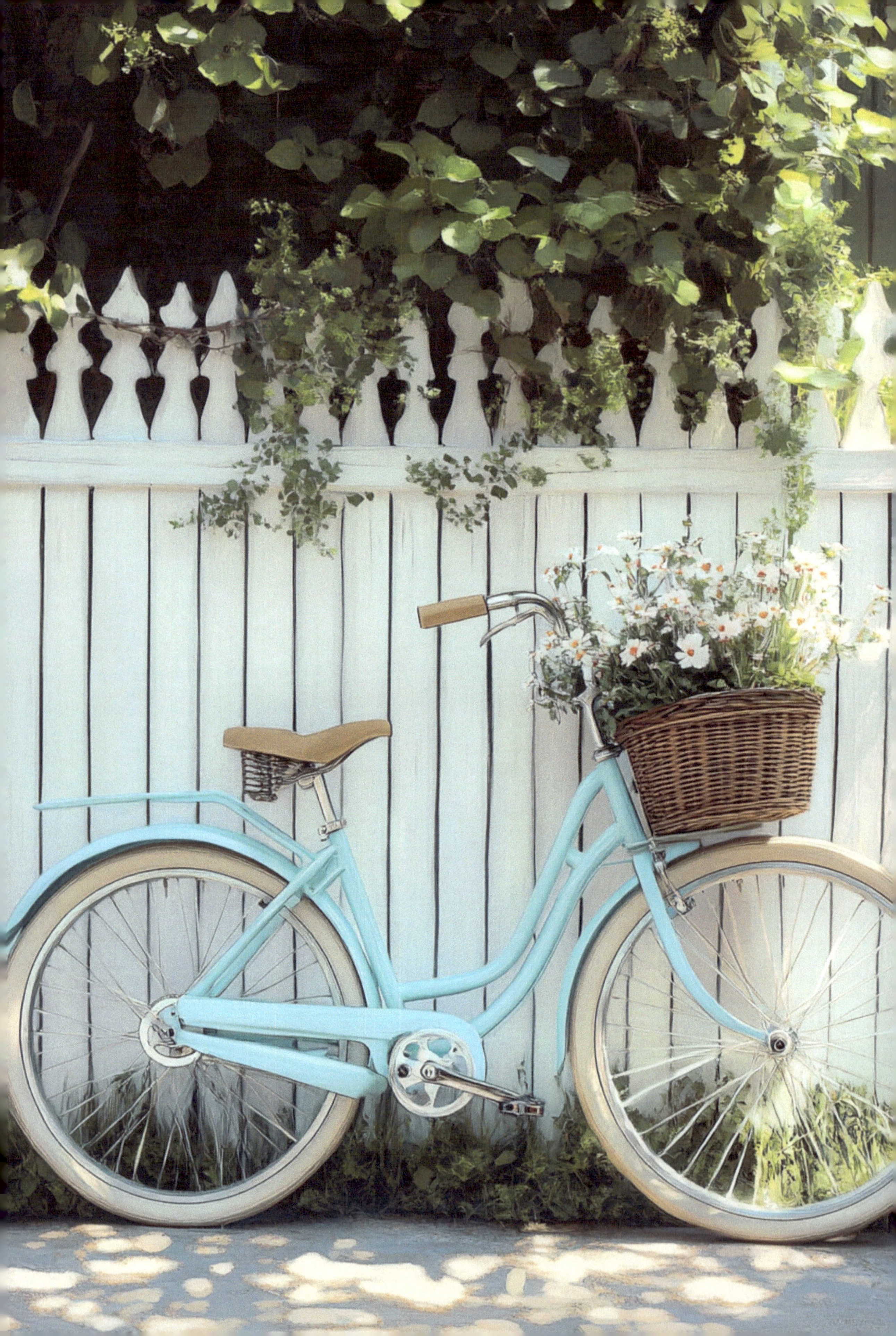

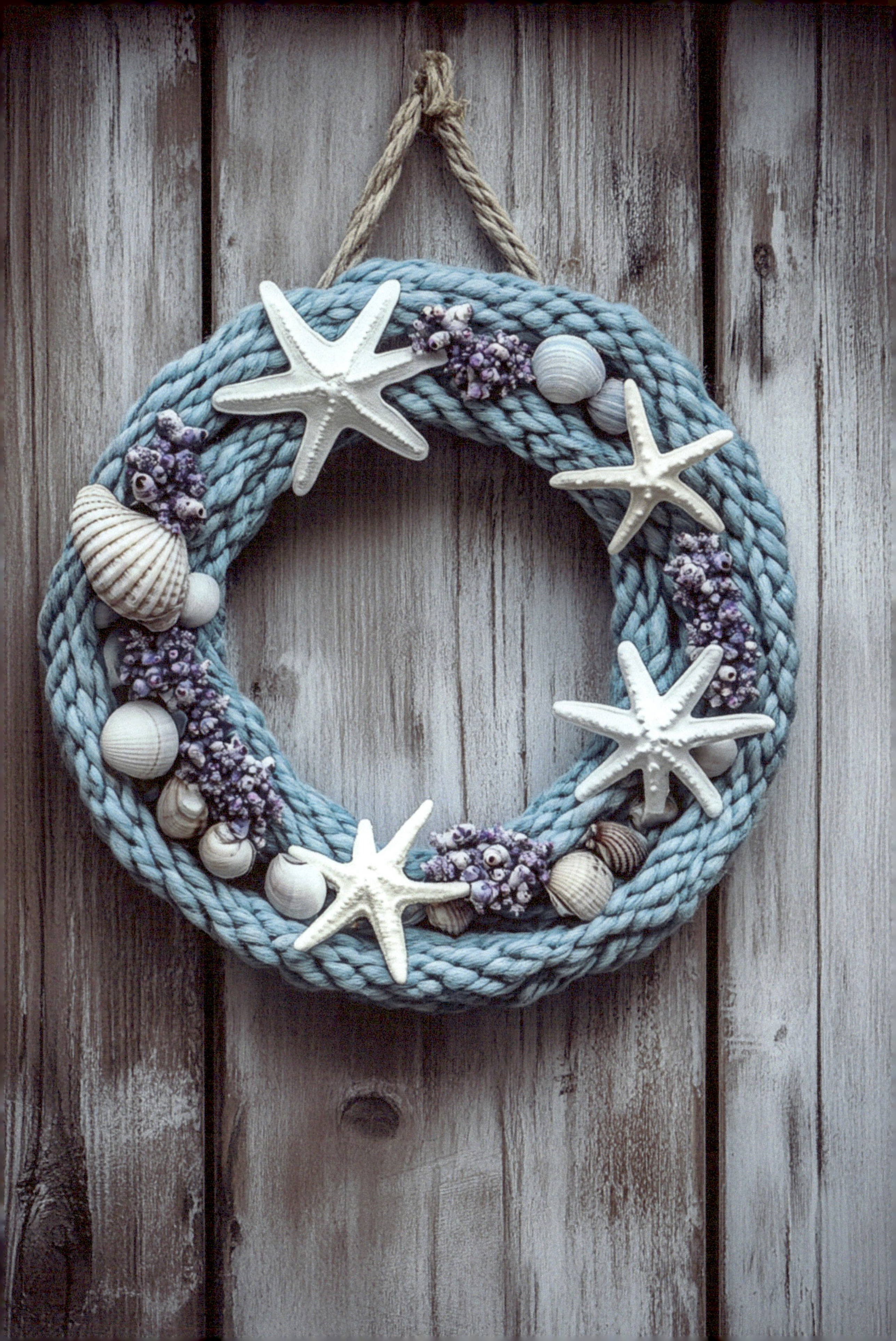

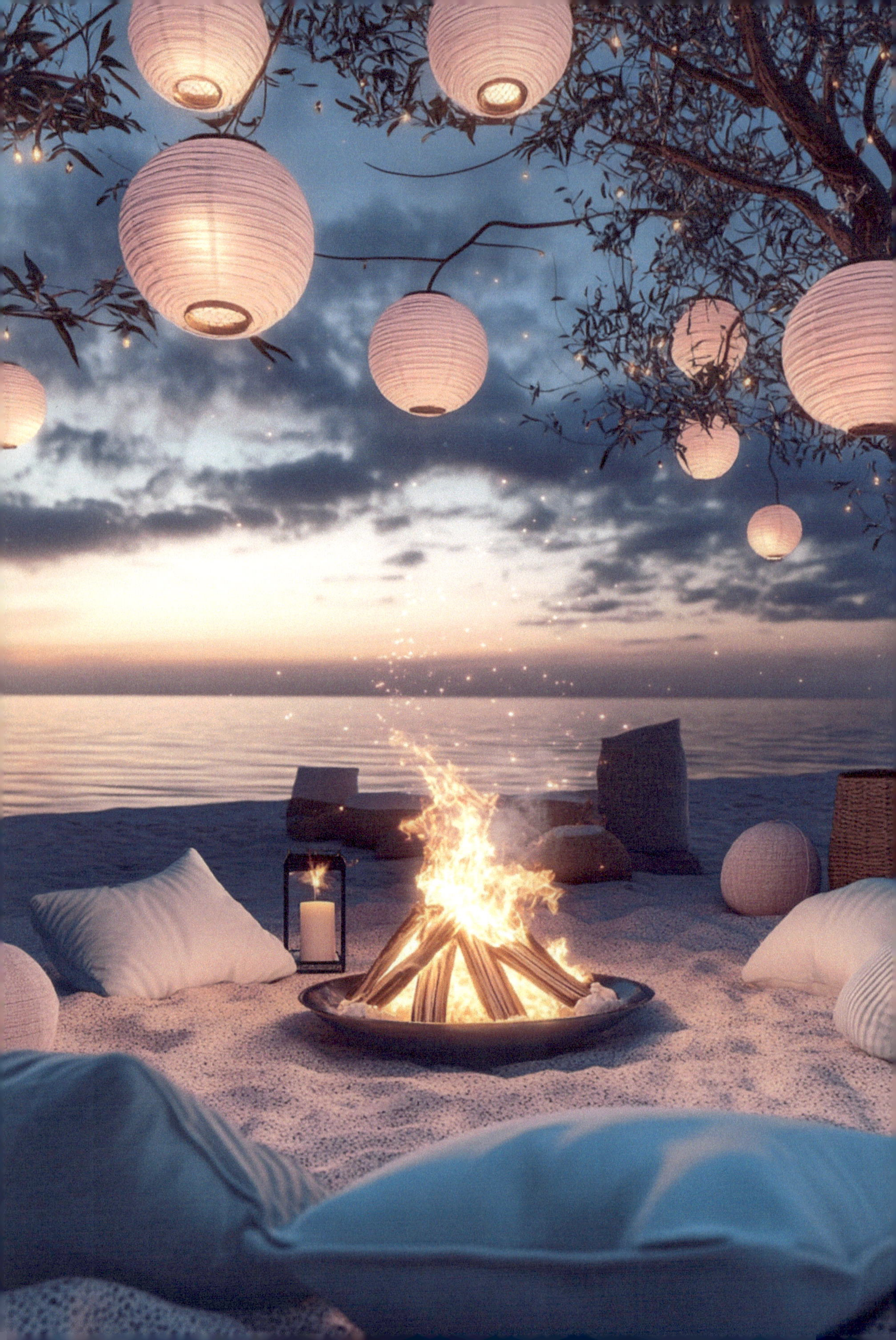

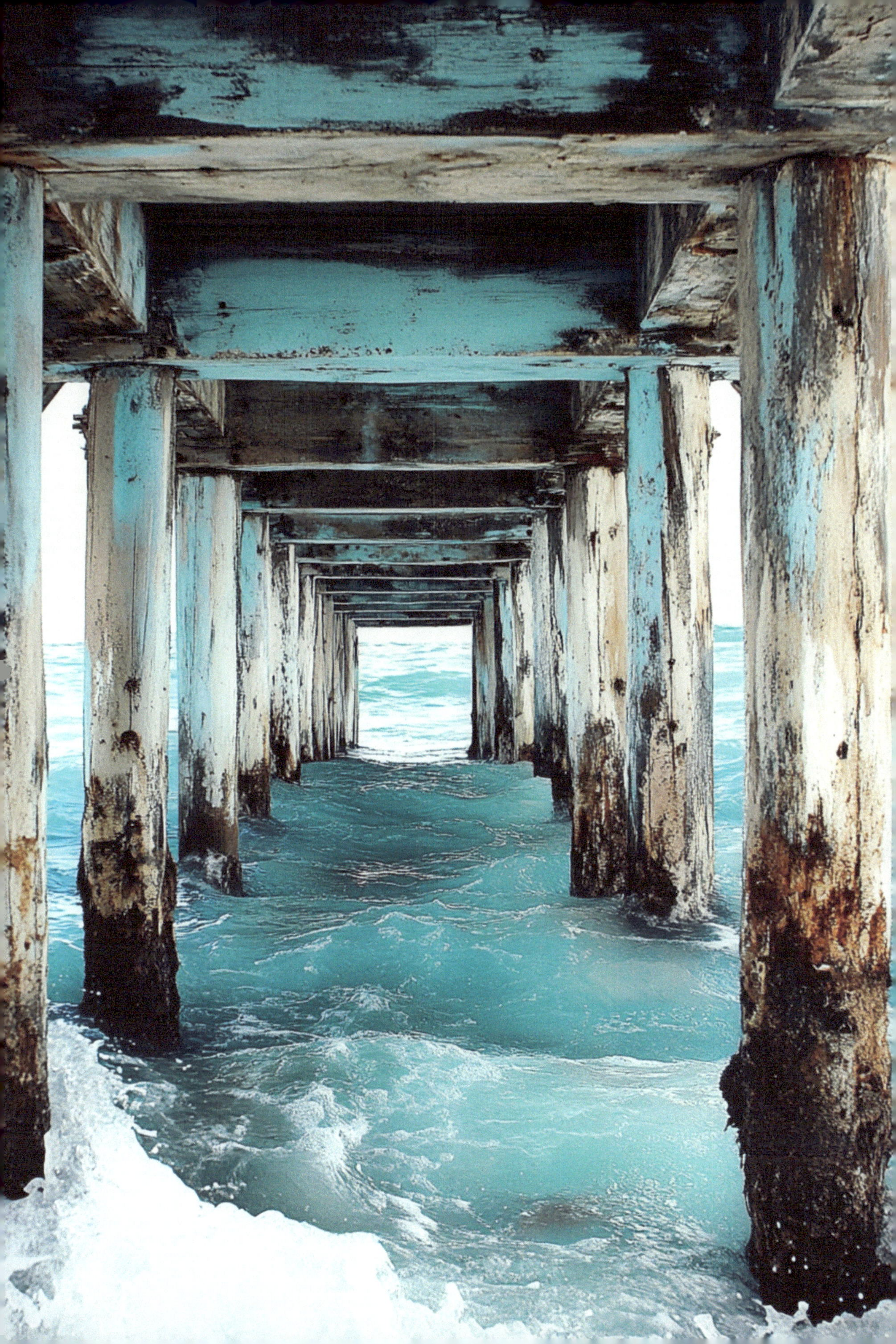

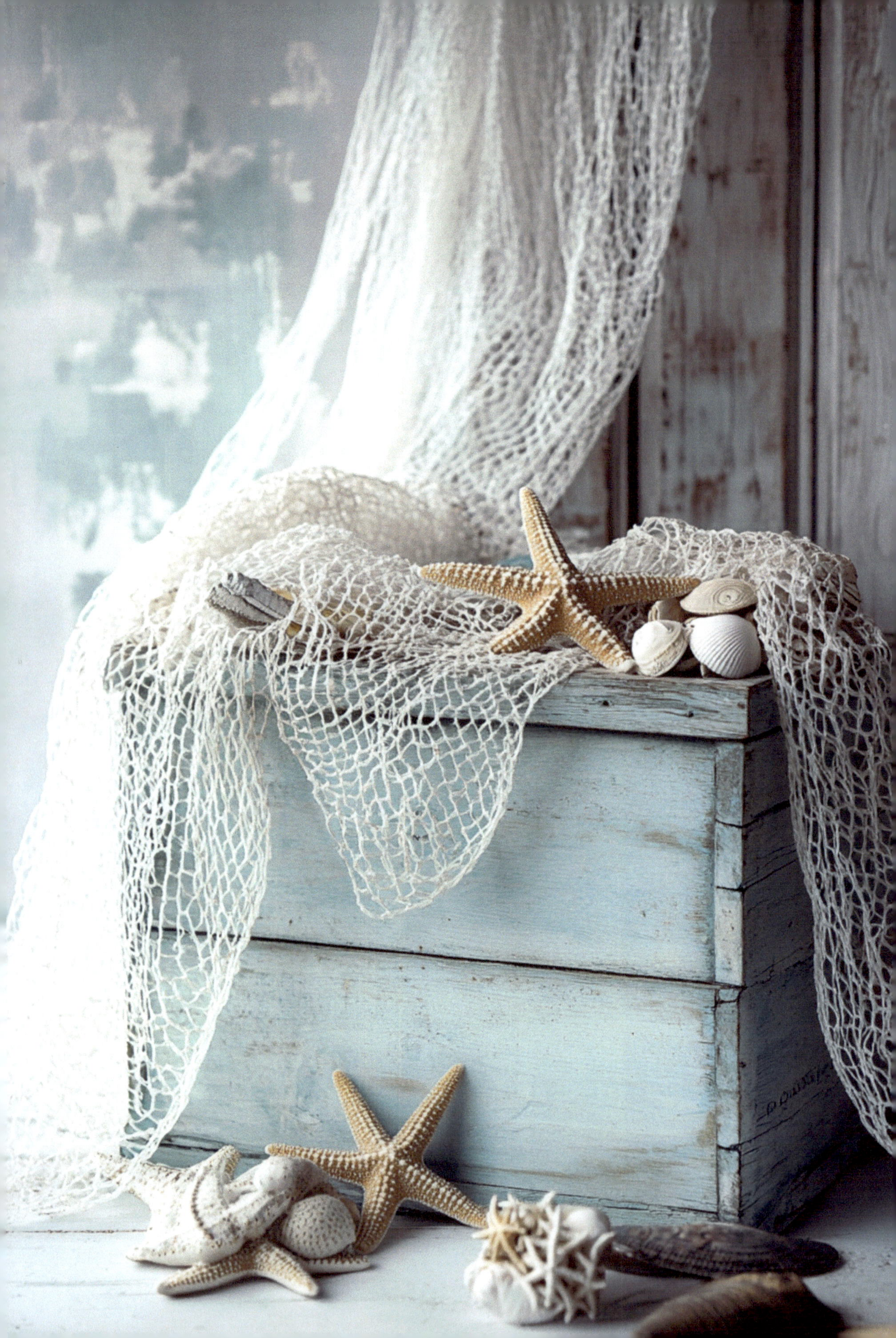

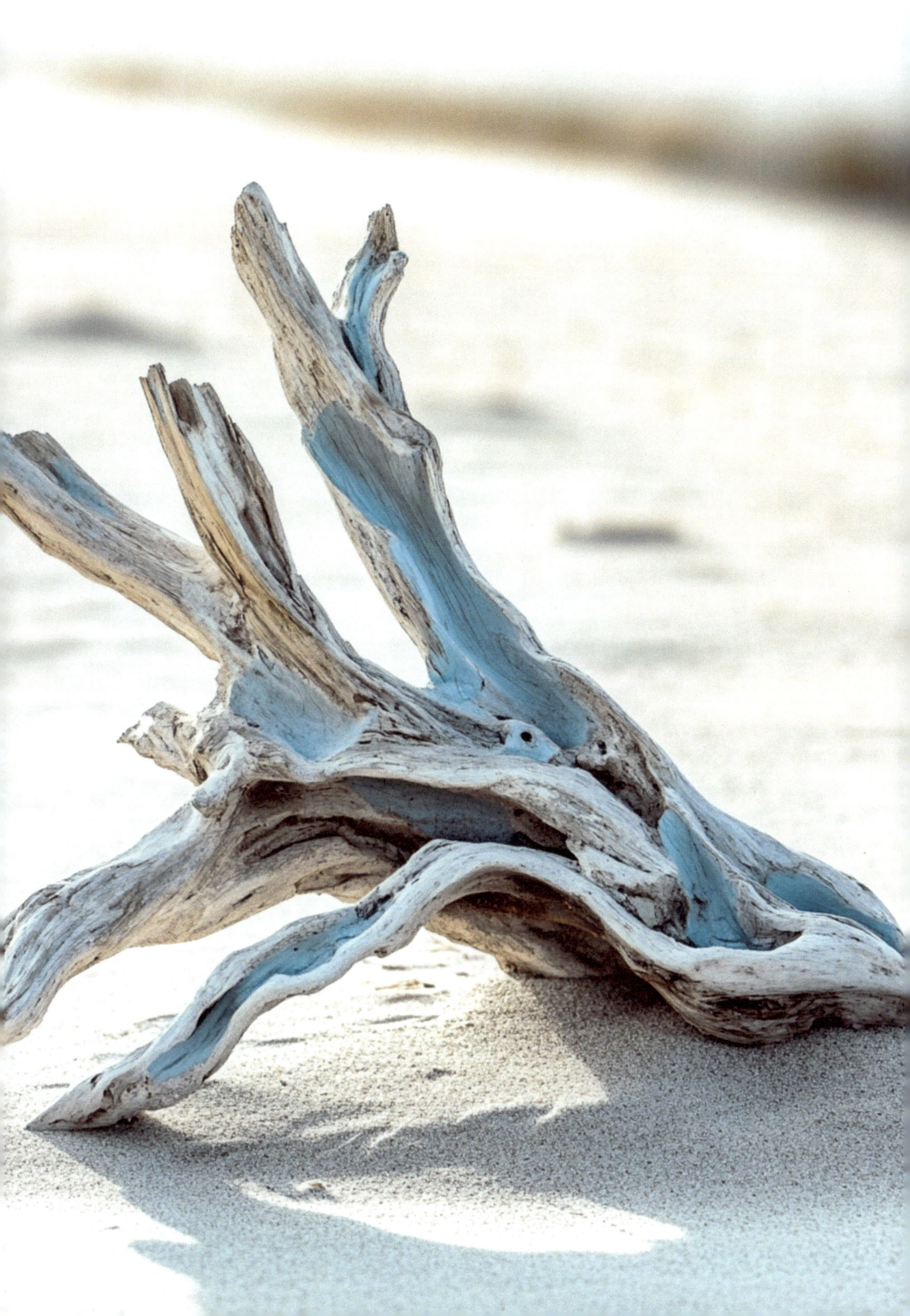

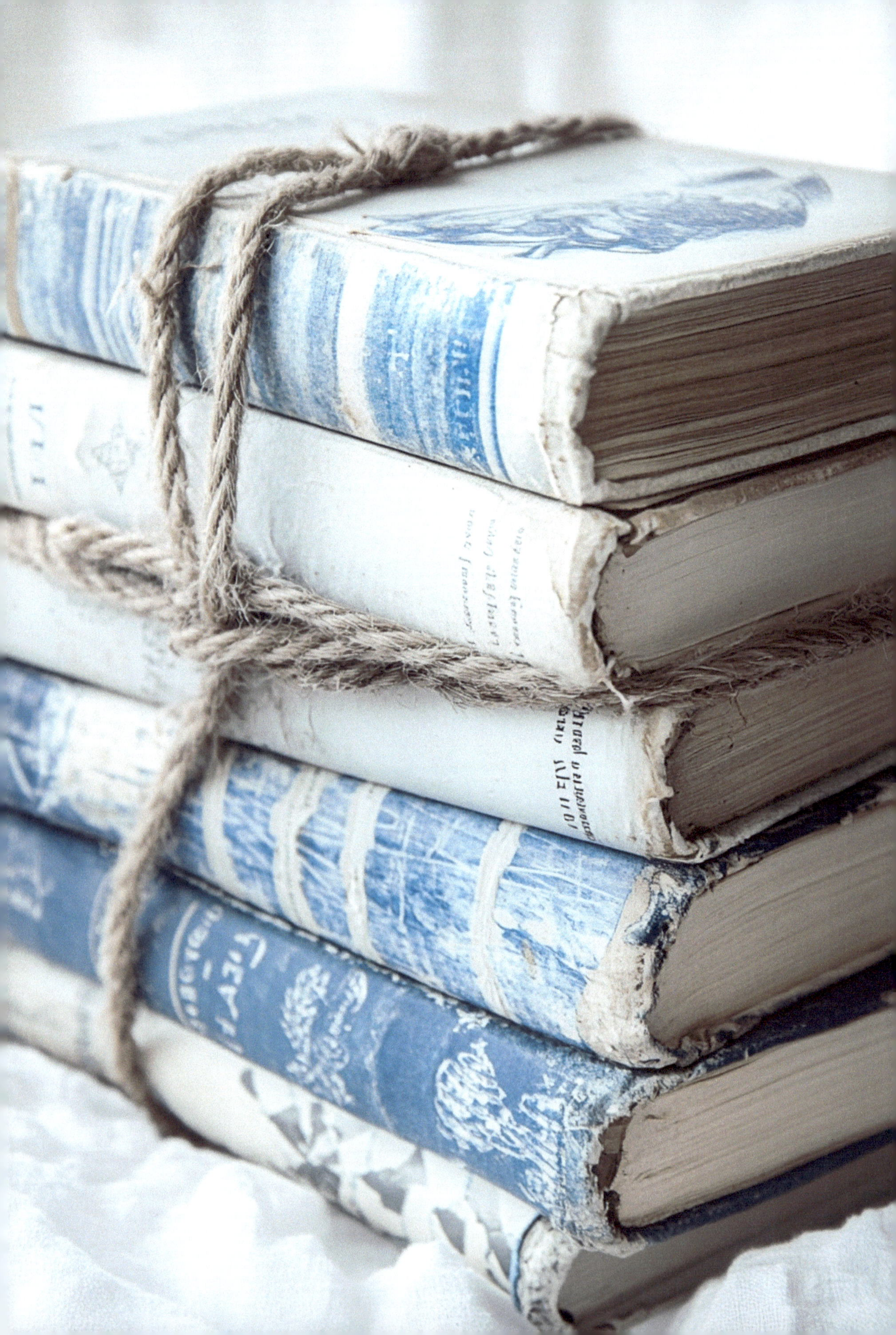

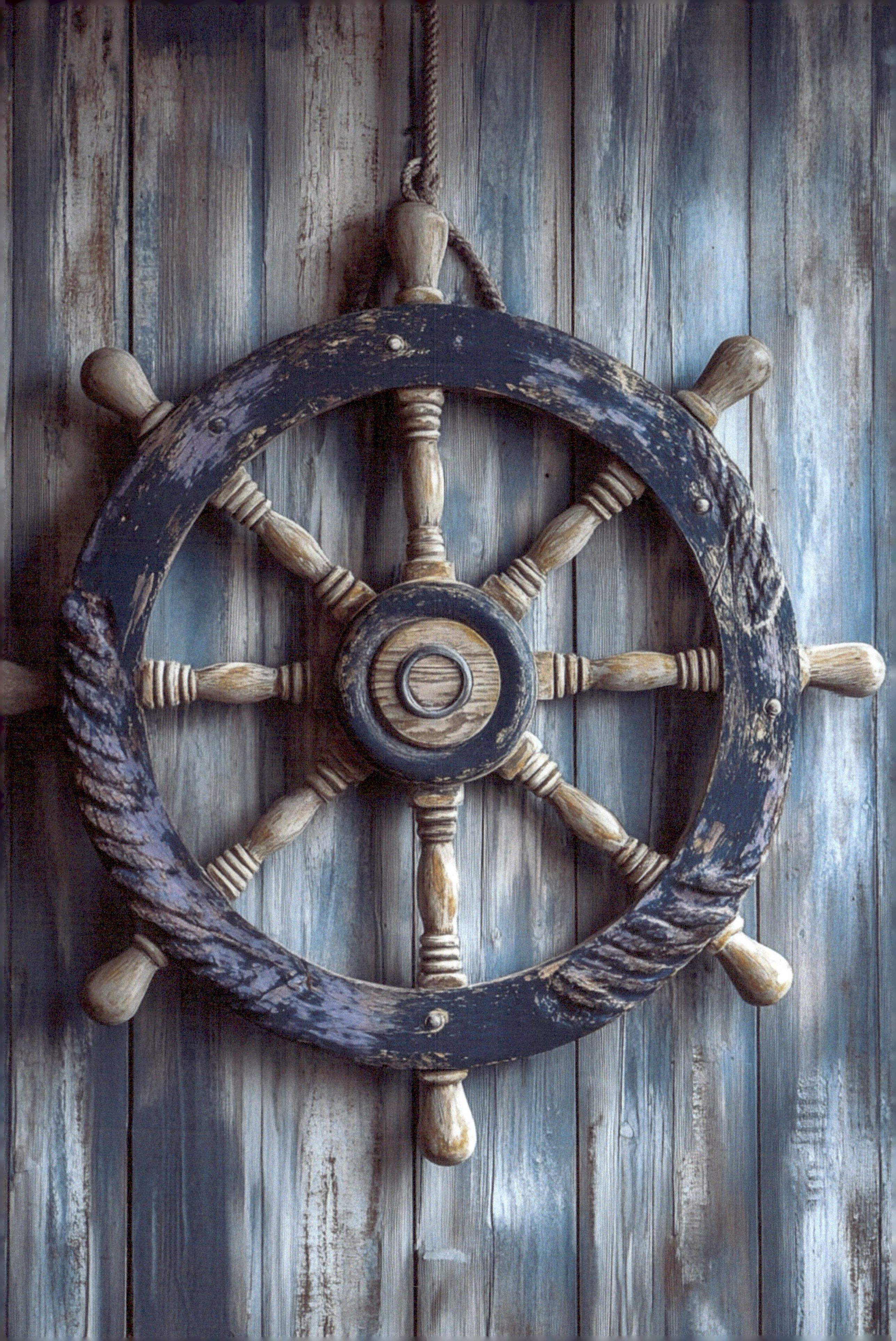

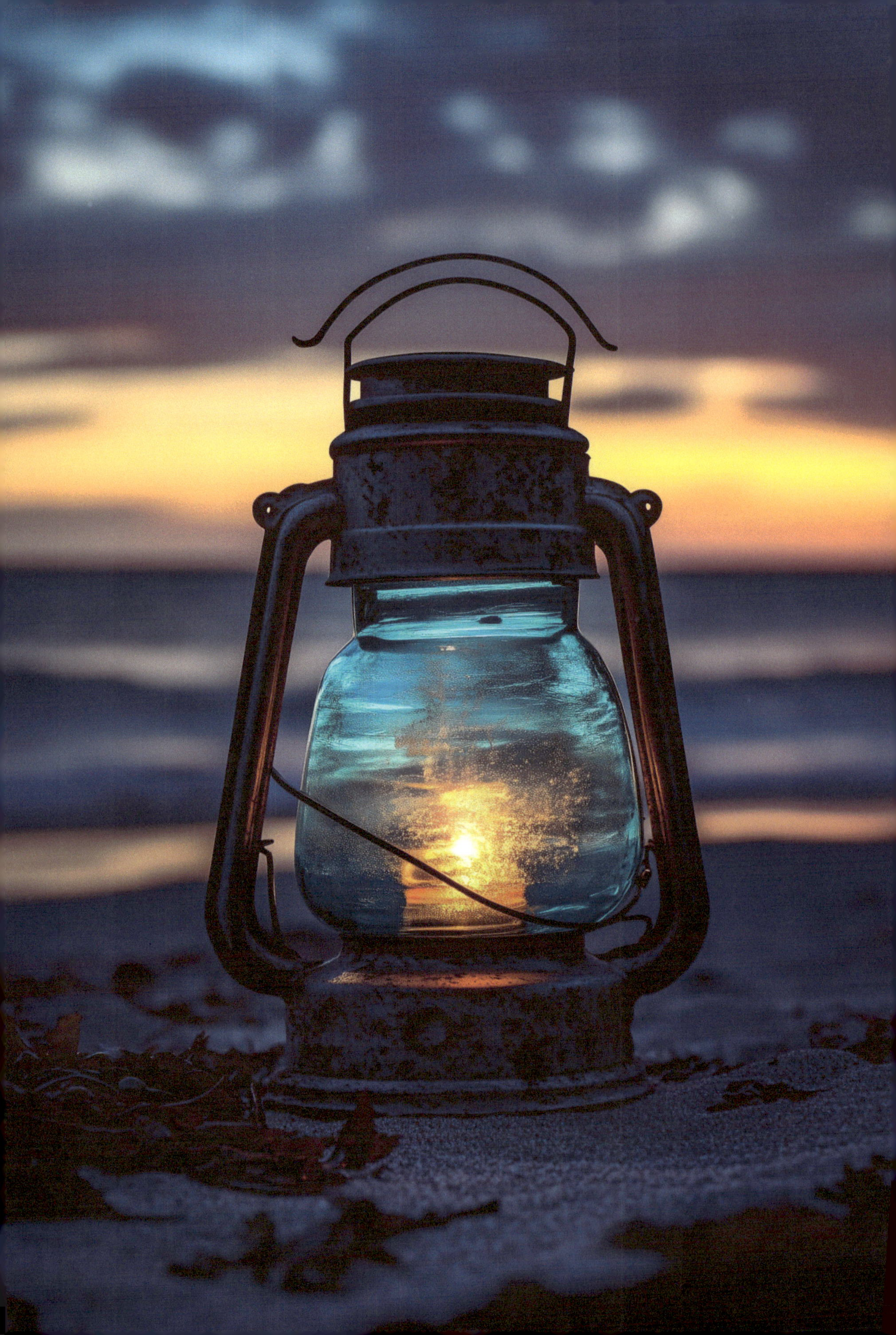

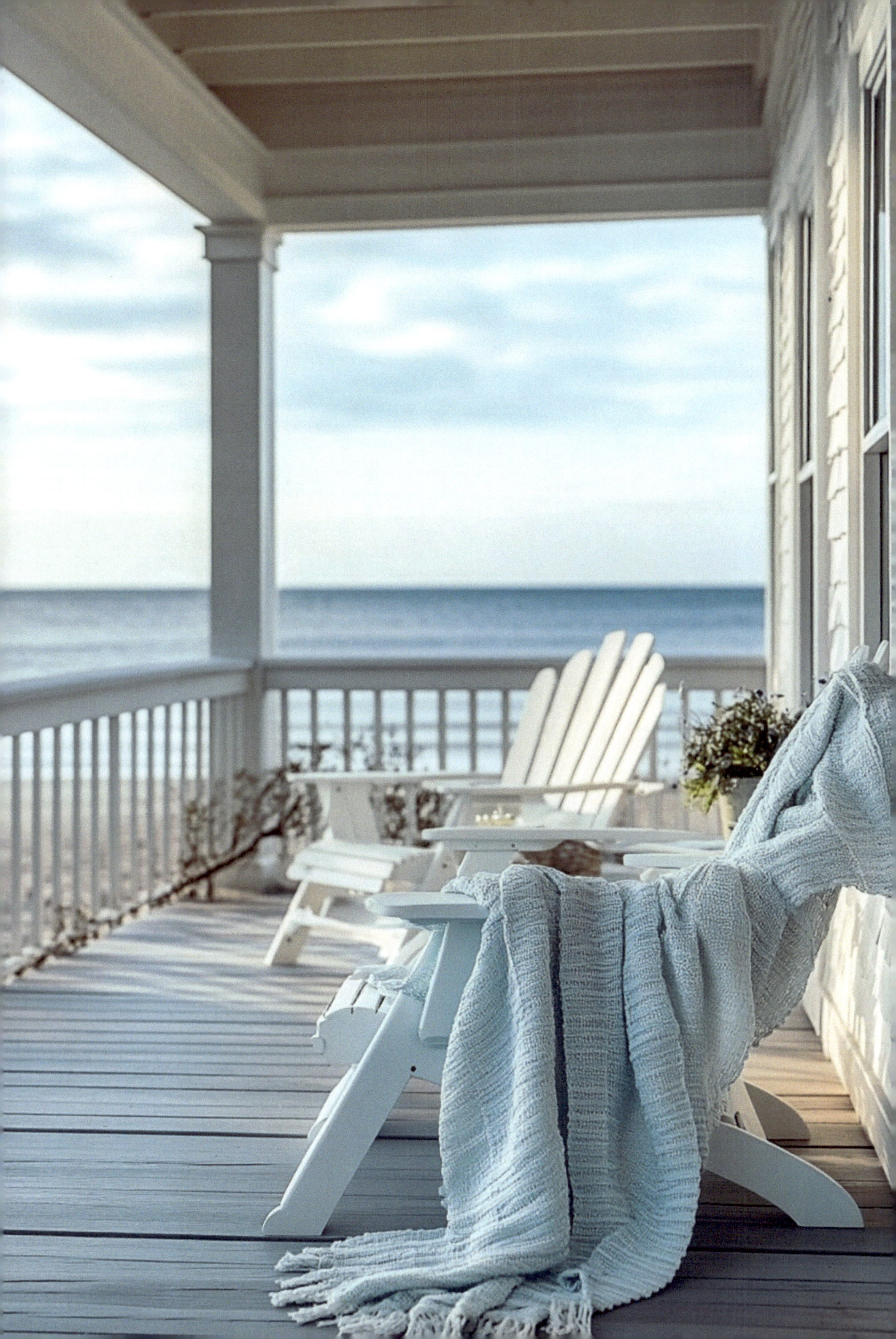

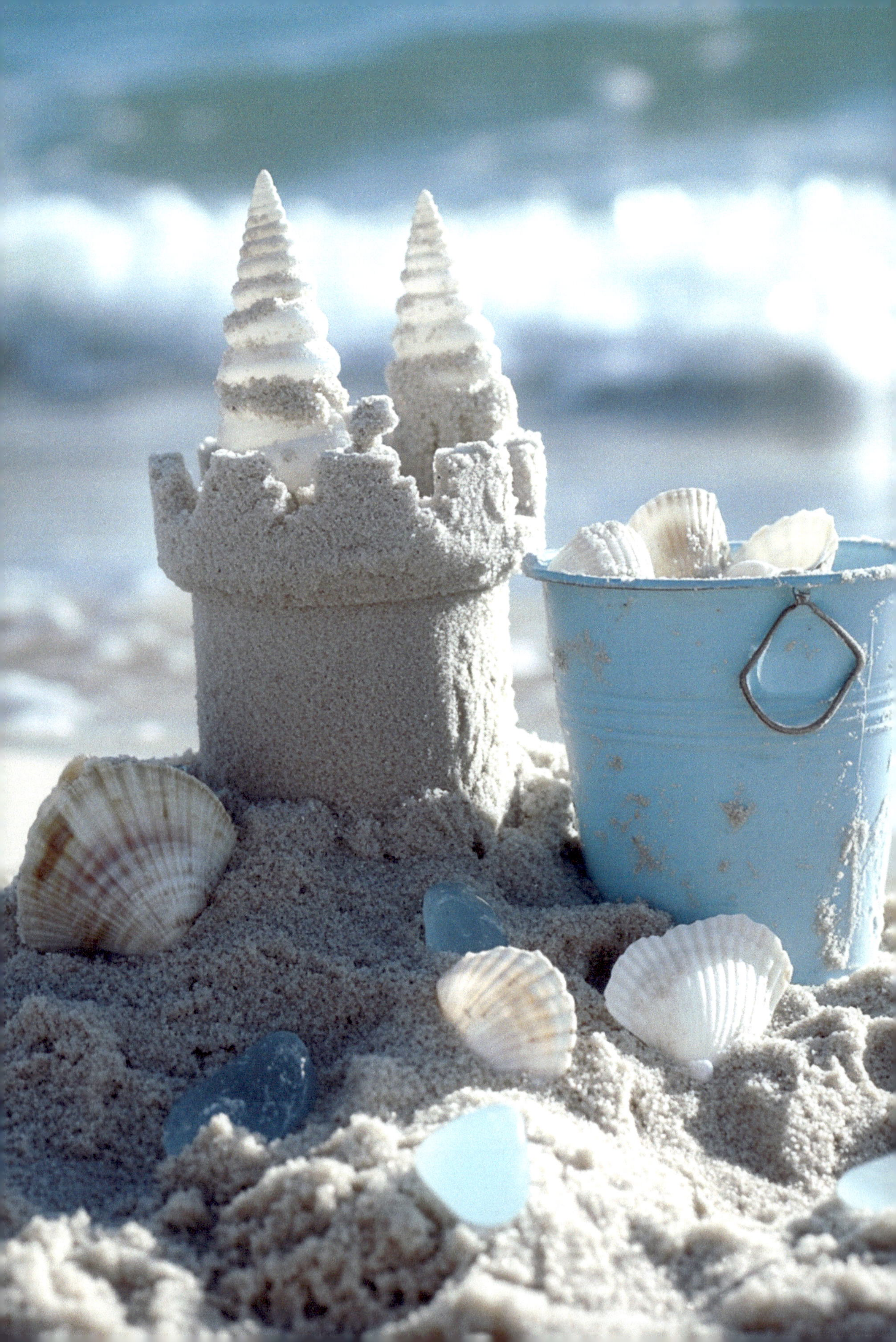

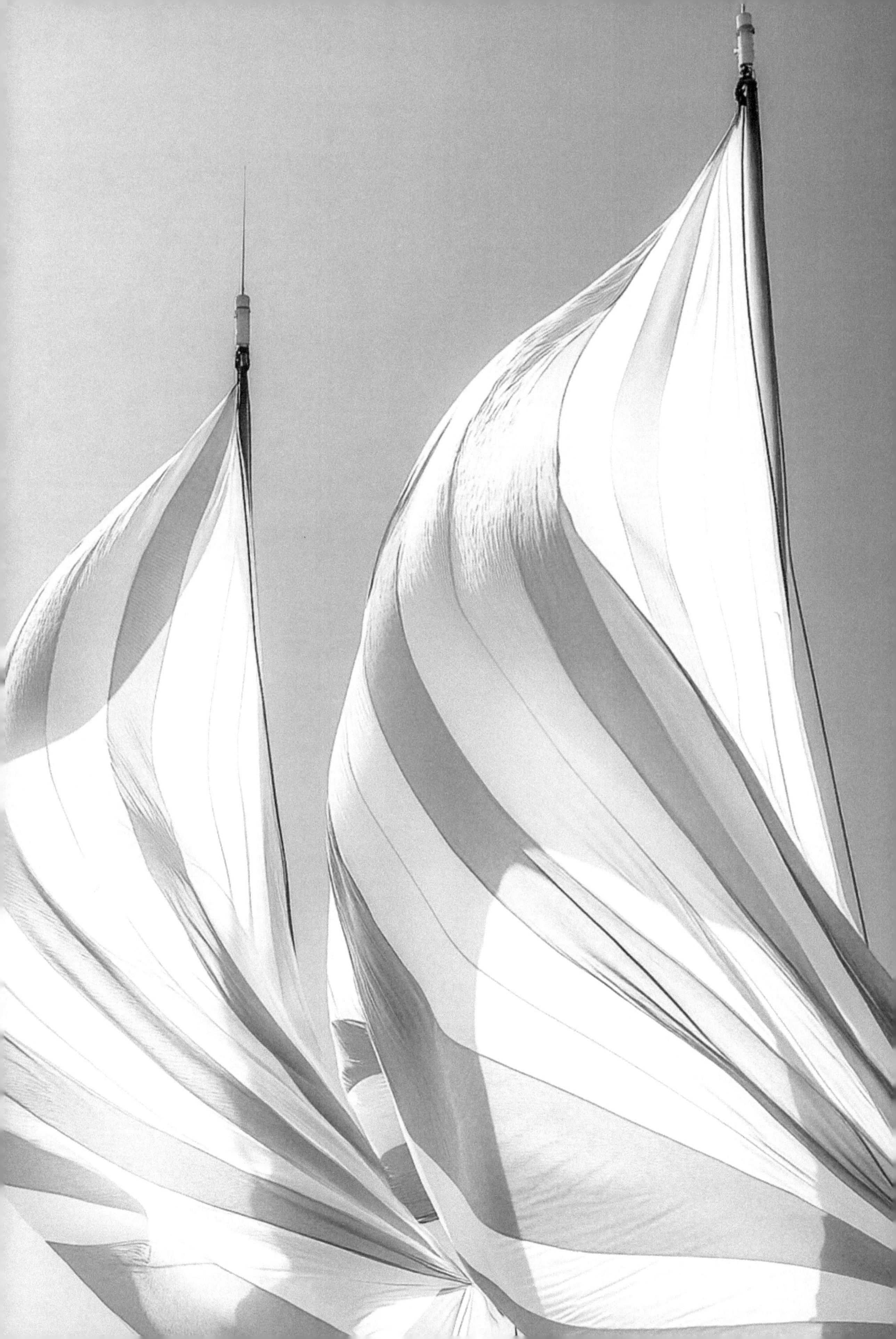

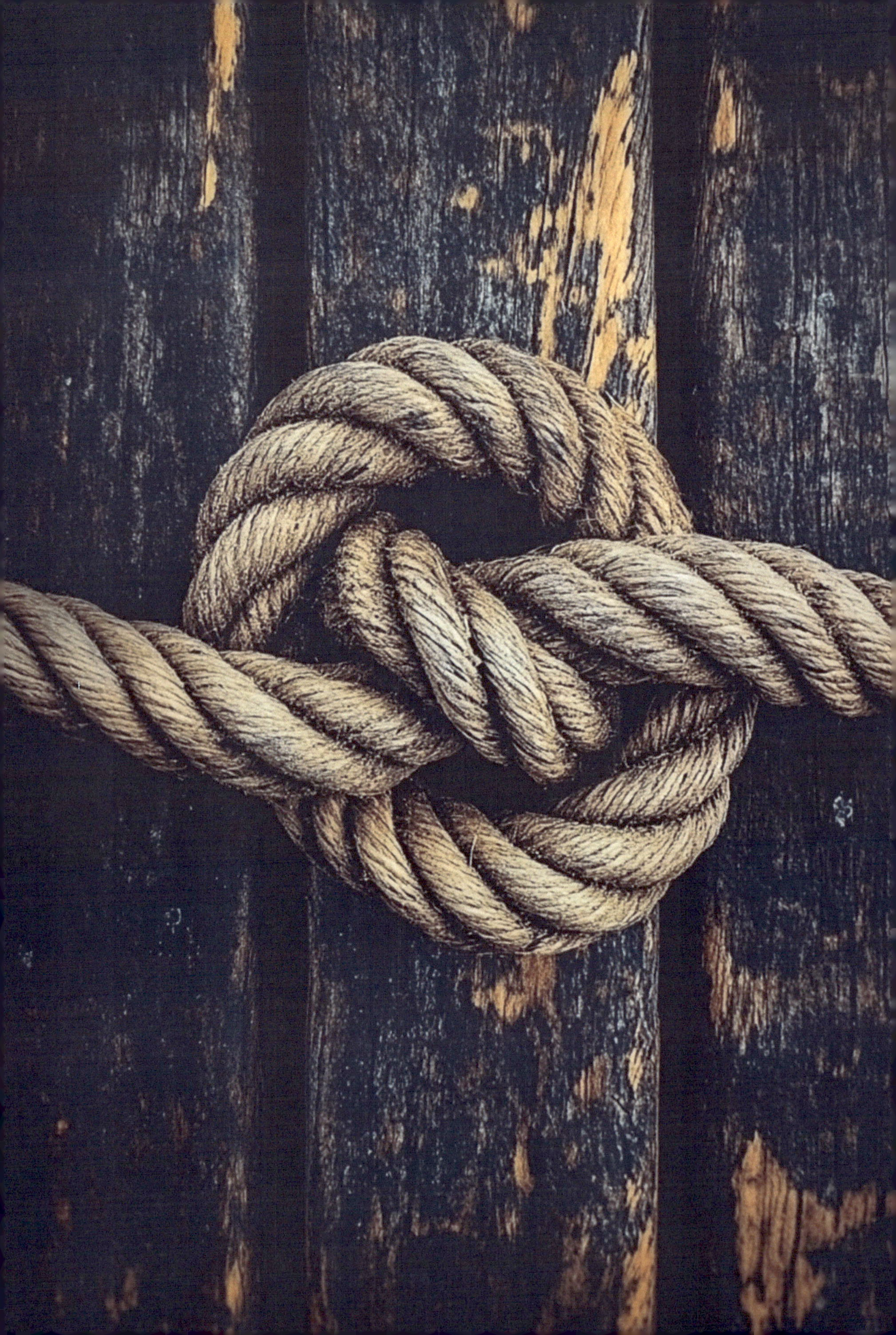

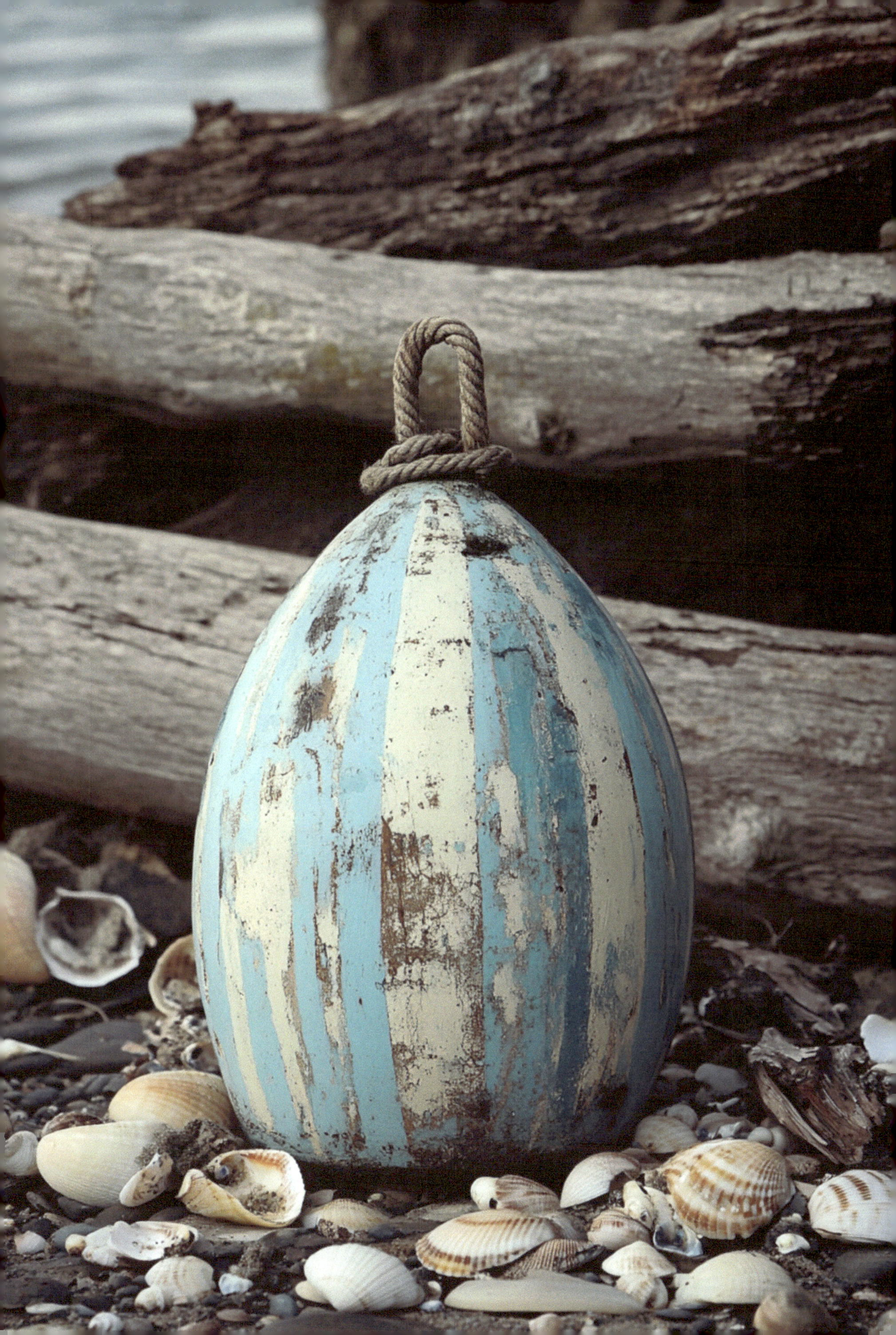

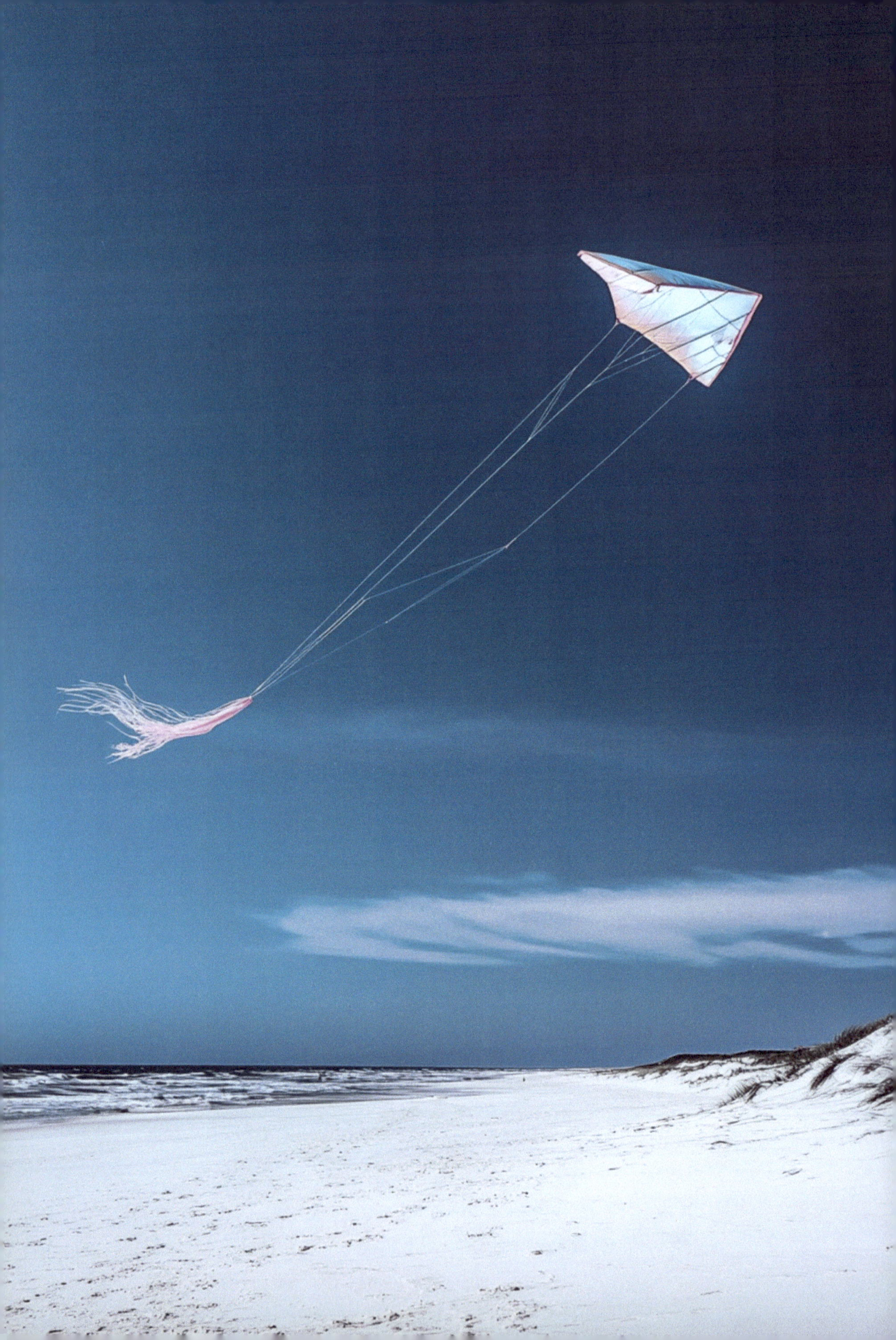

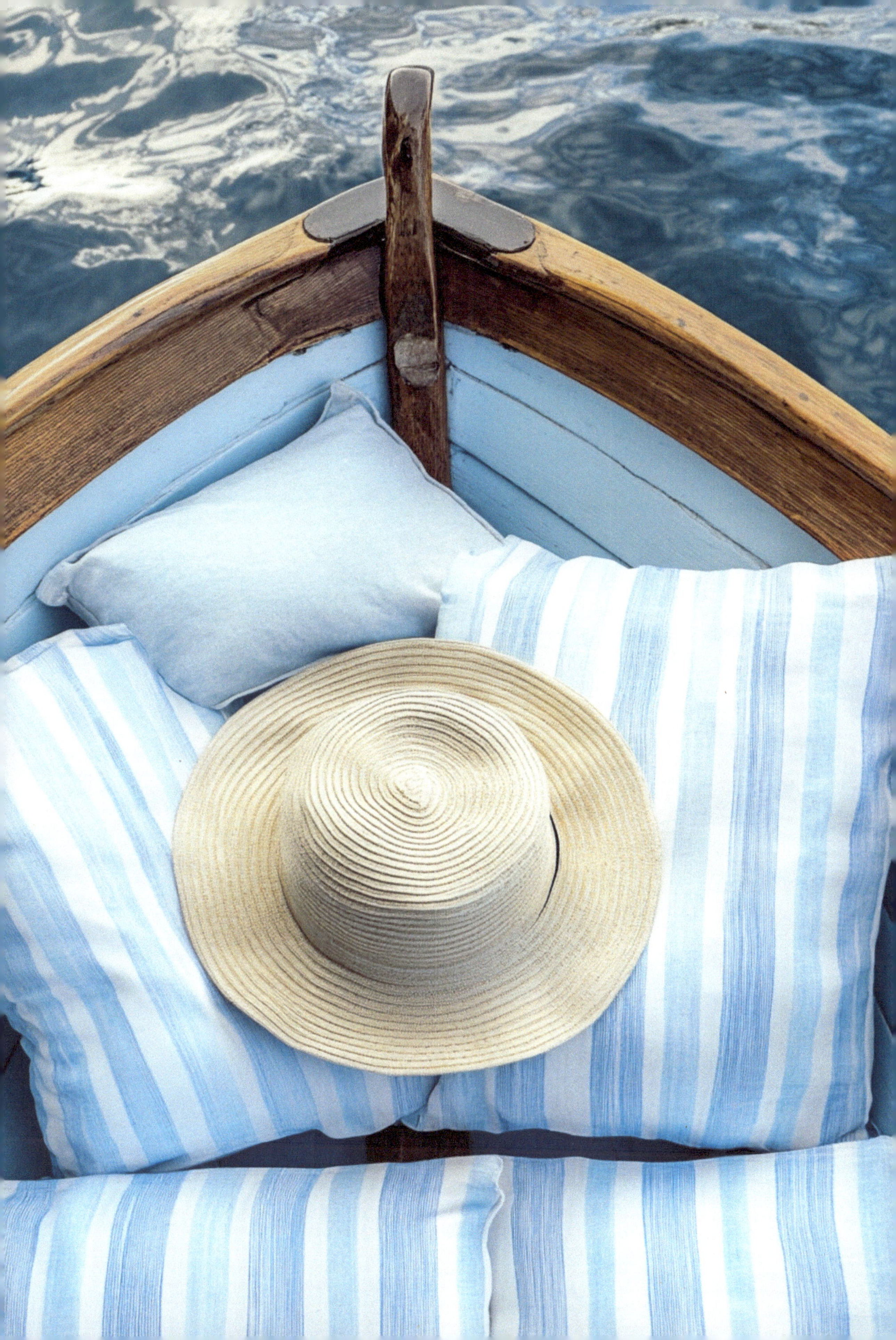

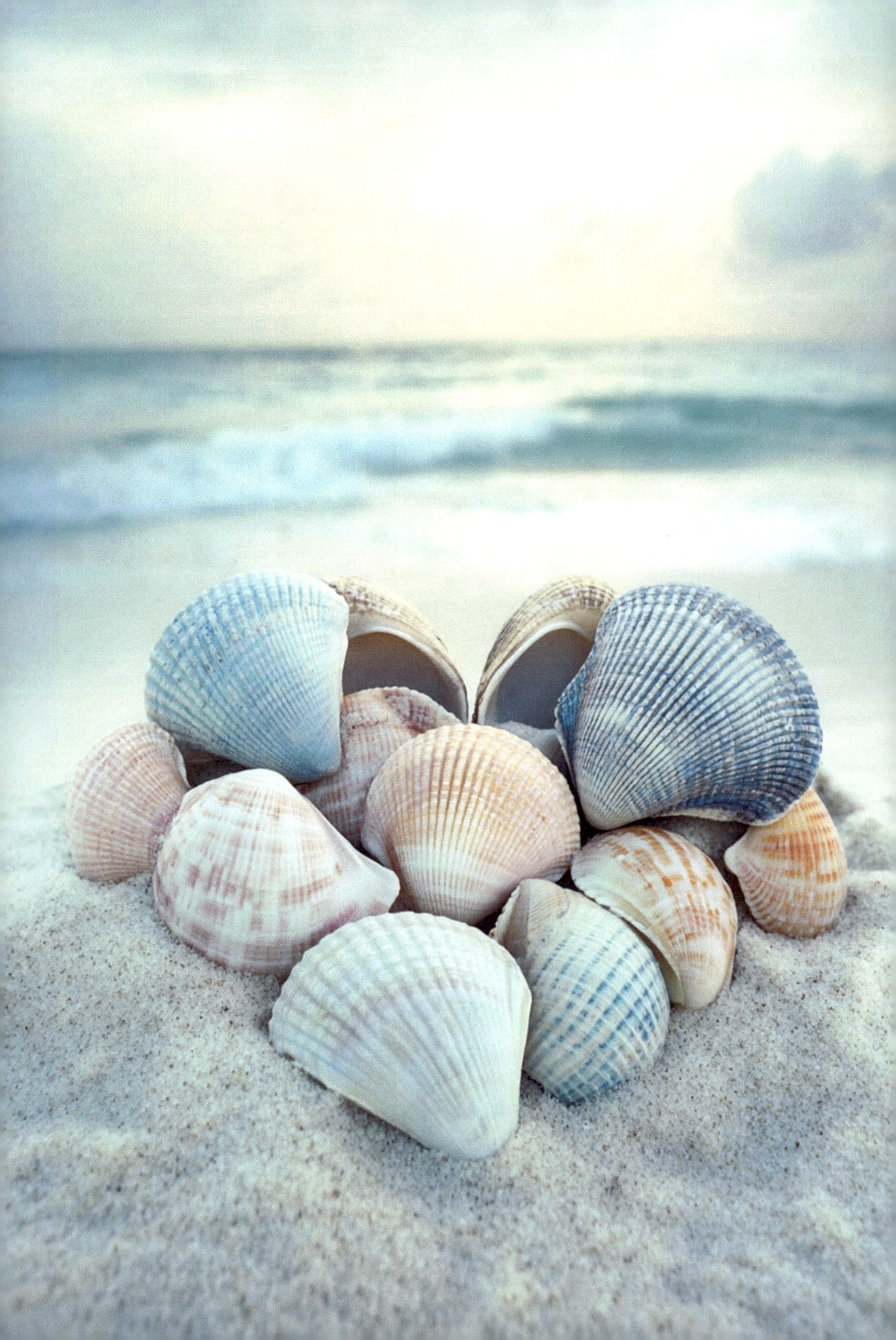

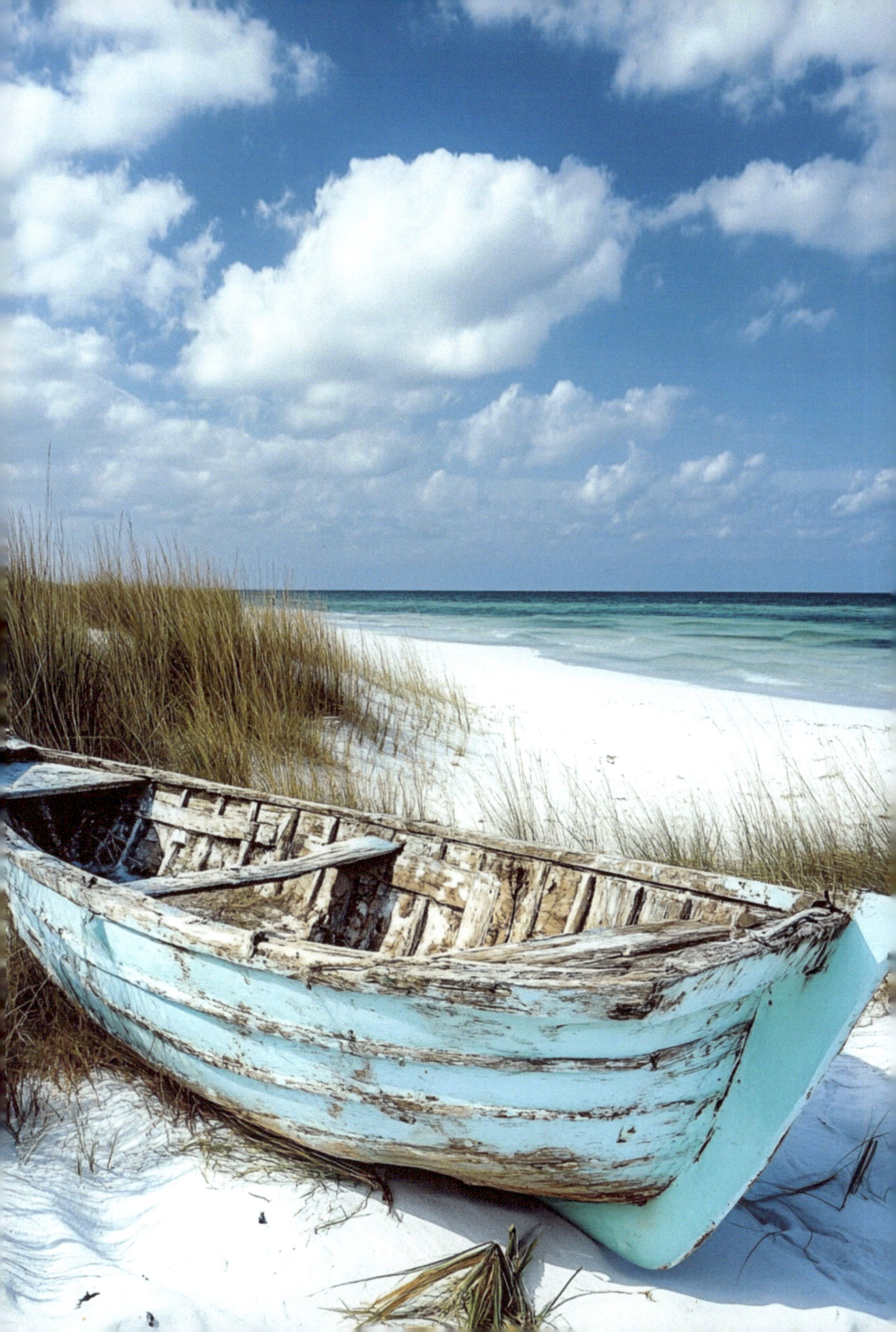

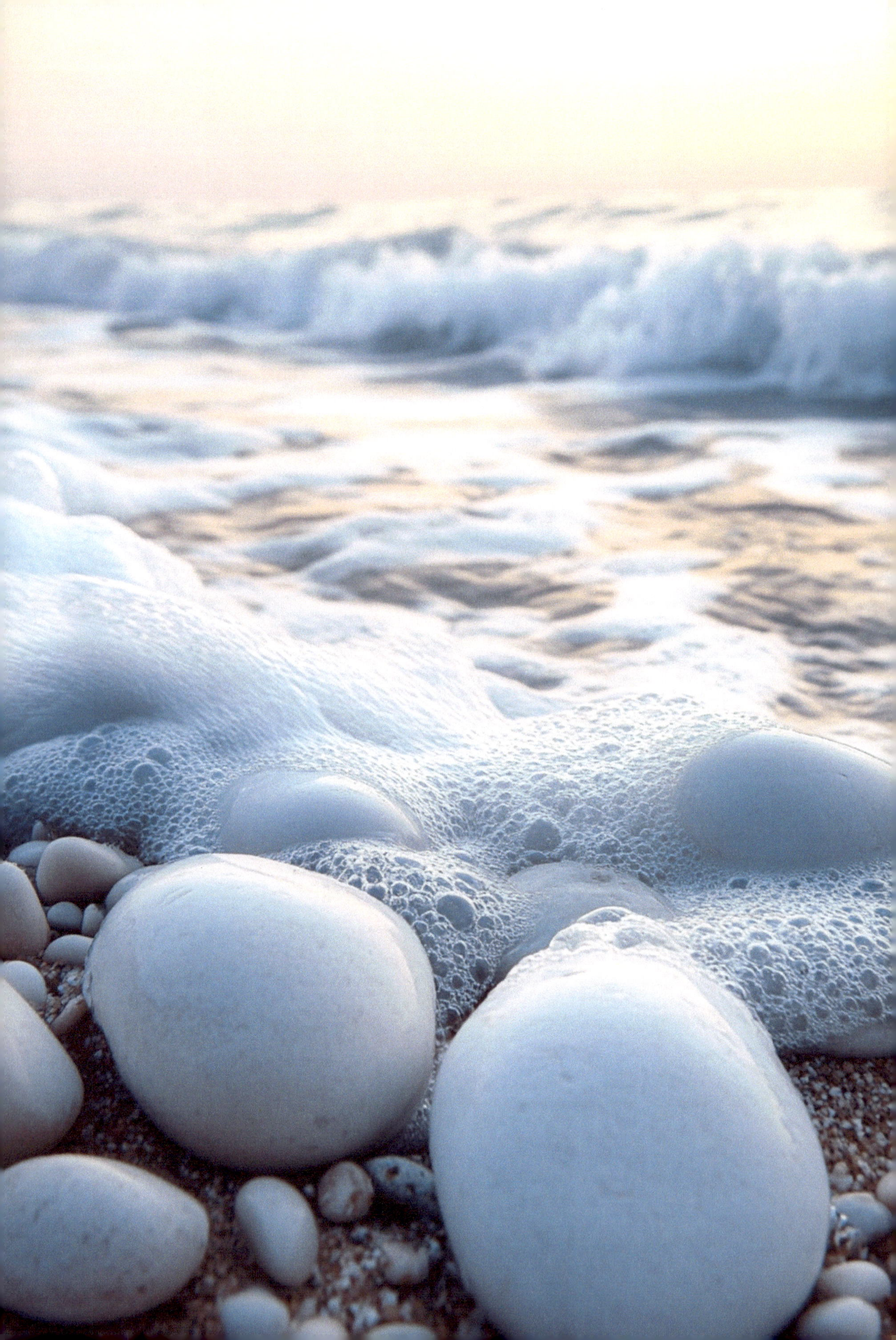

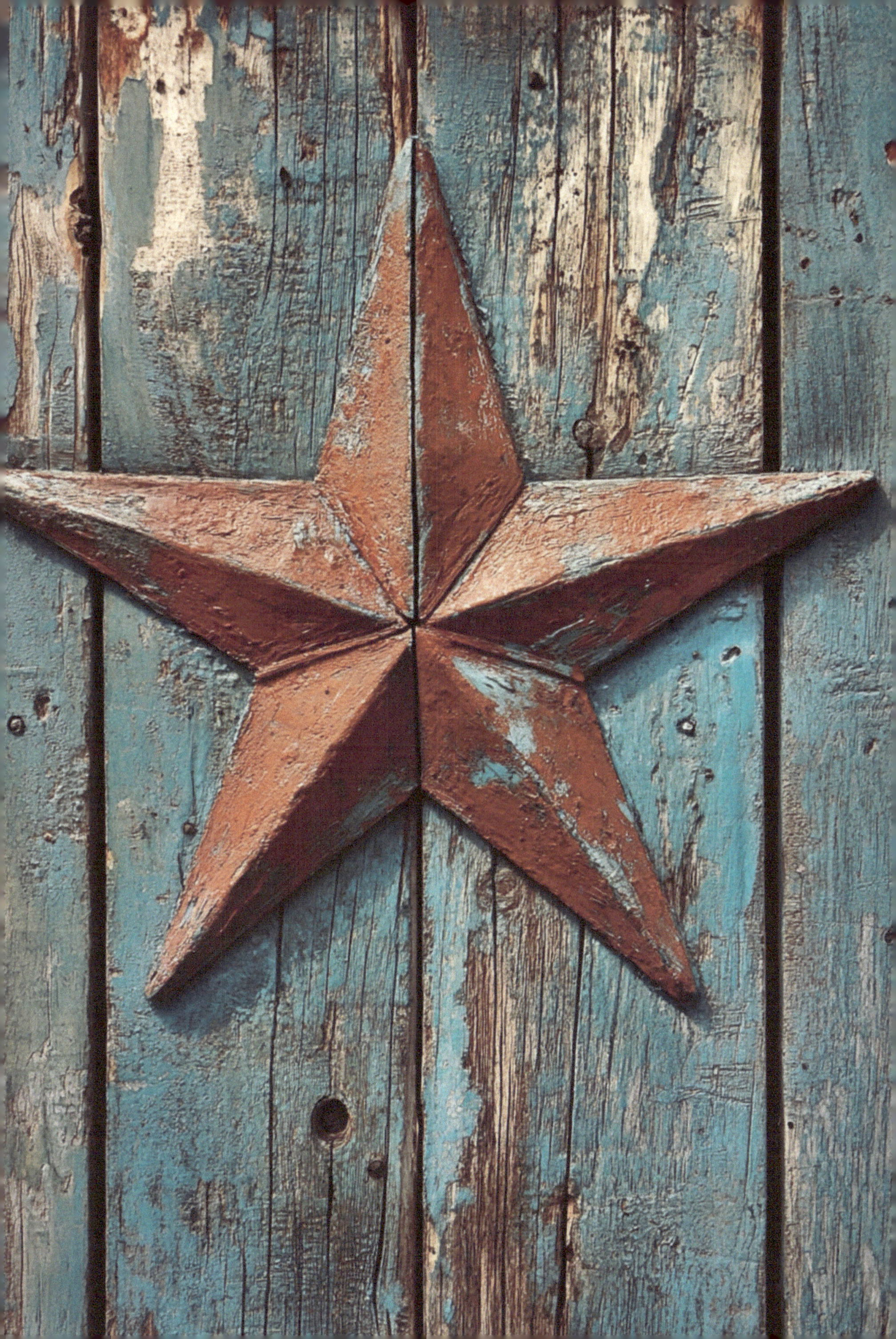

Other Raeka Harding Books

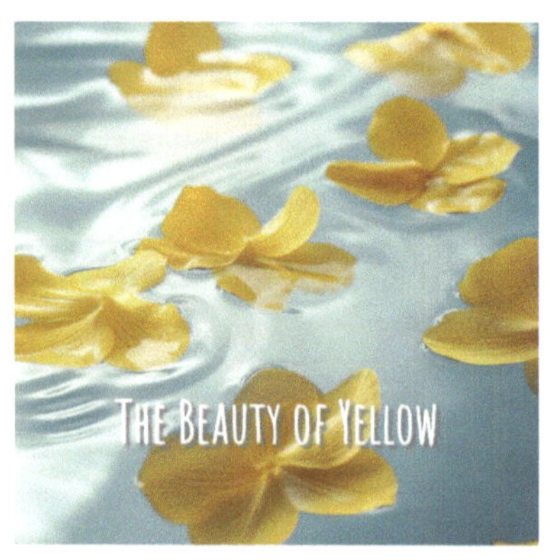

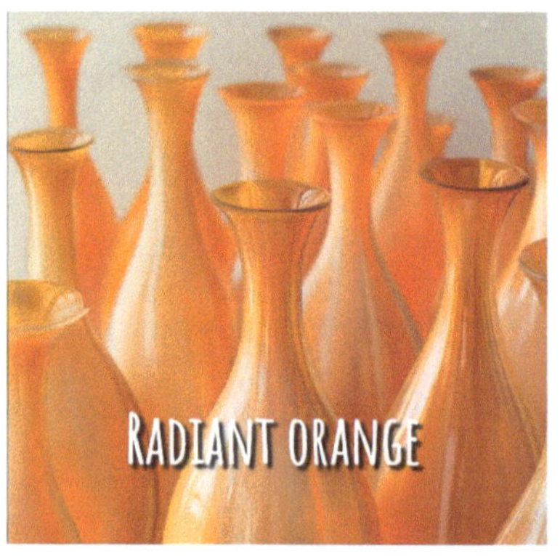

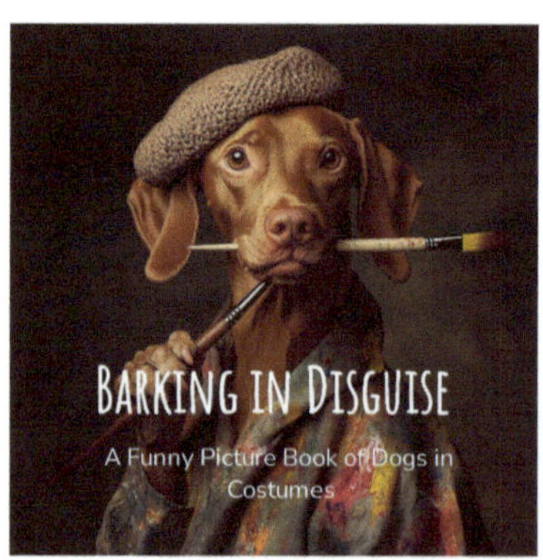

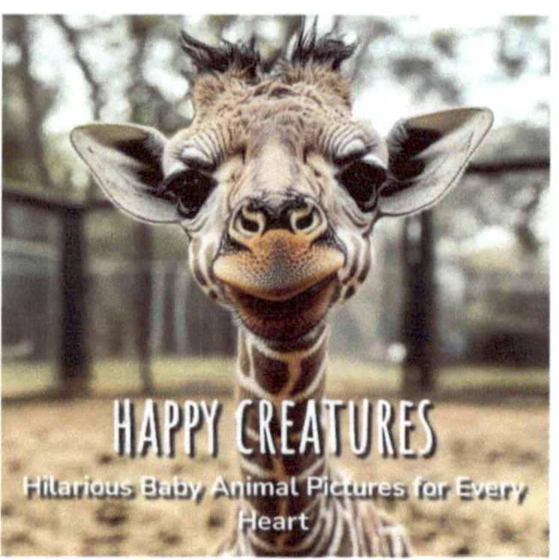